About the Author

Tamara Lloyd has had many and varied jobs and a whole host of qualifications in a number of different subjects but her life's ambition was always to dedicate herself to setting up an animal sanctuary and even though many obstacles were put in her way and there was a lot of stress in her life it was all worth it to get to her ultimate aim of helping as many animals in need as she could.

Dedication

To Shamus, Fowler, Walter and Kira who I let down badly and to all my other early animals whom I learned so much from. To those human supporters who have gone some way to showing me that there are some genuine, good souls out there who do care about animals.

Tamara Lloyd

THE ALTERNATIVE ANIMAL SANCTUARY

Animals I have known

AUSTIN MACAULEY
PUBLISHERS LTD.

ISBN 978 1 78455 296 1 (Paperback)
ISBN 978 1 78455 298 5 (Hardback)

www.austinmacauley.com

First Published (2015)
Austin Macauley Publishers Ltd.
25 Canada Square
Canary Wharf
London
E14 5LB

Printed and bound in Great Britain

Visit **www.alternativesanctuary.co.uk**

Contents

Chapter I

Sanctuary – The Beginnings

The Alternative Sanctuary started on a very small scale when we took in a few unwanted animals while living in a small semi-detached house in Carpenters Park Watford. Our first cat was a young female found at the stables where we kept our two horses. No one would take her on, so after feeding her for a while we caught her. The youngest of my three sisters was told to take her into the house and tell my dad how desperately she wanted to keep her. He accepted it pretty well as he did the few hundreds (maybe even into the thousands by now) that followed! Suzie as we named her had to become Suza when the vet discovered that she was a he! He moved houses with us later but always remained quite nervous.

Our first rescued horse we brought for £50 (the knacker price). He had been a blood horse at a racing yard, (he had blood taken from him regularly to give to the valued and cared for racehorses) he was only four years old and had been brought by a man for his daughter. When feed prices became terribly expensive (because there was a grain shortage) he was due to be shot. Because so many people could no longer afford to keep their horses – so many were being shot – he was kept waiting for three days locked in a stable for the knacker man. On the third day my mother couldn't stand it anymore so she bought him. He had anaemia from losing so much blood so had to be given Guinness and my mother had to go to the stables three times a day to give him small feeds. He also had to have salt rubbed into his gums to strengthen them as he had a 'parrot mouth' – a deformed jaw so that the top overshot the bottom and made it difficult for him to eat. As he got stronger he became difficult to handle and it was discovered that he had not been properly gelded (castrated.) One testicle had not descended so he had to have a fairly major operation to sort that out.

Our first rescued dog was Sunday who one of my sisters found while out on a horse ride. She was an Airedale and totally doolally. It took hours to catch her. She was partly nervous, partly disobedient and as she got older she became deaf and blind. She gave my sister many embarrassing moments going through people's dustbins and refusing to come when called. She was named Sunday as we found her on a Sunday!

It would take too long to go through all of the histories of the animals we took in but these were really the founding cases. We moved to a bigger house in Garston, Watford and rented two fields. My father put up some make-shift stables in one of the fields (the first of many).

With the house we brought three ponies as the owner was a dealer and threw them in as part of the deal! We have been advised this was not normal practice! One was to be my first pony Ginger who spent most weekends throwing me off and leaving me with concussion, as he was not broken or backed – I was only six years old at the time! My two elder sisters had the others, Pedro and Warrior. Pedro was a grey and a wilful pony. He used to love to rub my sister up against trees, gates and hard surface and hear her scream as he trapped her leg. Warrior was a handsome 15.2hh cob.

Warrior was stolen with Connie, my second eldest sister's other pony, on her eighteenth birthday. They were never found despite numerous trips to Markets particularly notably Southall which still has an appalling reputation for how the animals are treated. We would all come away in tears each Wednesday as we saw so many poor souls we would have liked to have brought had we been able to. There were also the birds and goats being sold for ritual slaughter. The handlers would shout and beat the terrified horses most of whom were in a bad physical condition. On one visit I remember a horse with scars all up its legs from bandages applied too tightly, and a lovely bay cob with a curly coat, we now know to be the sign of Cushing's Disease. What also stuck in my mind was a gorgeous small child's pony who must have wondered how it came to be in such a hell hole. It had been immaculately groomed with shapes groomed into its hind quarters. We travelled the country for over a year looking for Connie and Warrior but years later we discovered that up the road from us was an illegal slaughterhouse where they probably ended up hours after they were stolen. The police had shown little interest when we reported the crime and actually were more interested in the horse trailer they stole at the same time which we really were not interested in. The only consolation was that they were not transported for miles which was small comfort for one of the worst events in our life.

My mother was also talked into buying a rabbit with the house; he was being kept in such a small cage that he could not sit up or turn around. He was named Arthur, as he had cost the owner half a crown. He was to live in a shed with the run of the garden and gained a friend called Annabel (a male also!) he would attack everyone who tried to catch him except for my four year old brother. He was sent out each night to go and call him into the shed because everyone else was scared of him! My mother still has a scar the length of her inner arm from the time she tried to pick him up! Finally in our new home we discovered that we had inherited a cat that responded to the name Tinkerbell. The previous owners of the house had a cat called Tinkerbell, they would call Tinkerbell in for night and when Mog (that seemed more appropriate) tried to come in as well, the door was slammed swiftly in his face. After we moved in he was very happy to find that he was now allowed to come into the comfort of the house! He unfortunately got run over on the road directly outside our house, but thankfully only sustained a broken leg. He was kept in a rabbit hutch for six weeks which he hated. The idea being that this would enable his leg to heal. Sadly this was not to be the case and he managed for the rest of his life with a leg which had a distinctly unique angle to it. He found this to have an added advantage in that he could sit on top of the TV where it was nice and warm and hang it over the front so that it draped in front of the screen to ensure that no one could see properly! Whenever we took in a new cat, usually as the result of saving them from being put down at the vets, Mog would take them on an adventure to the A405 where the next day they would be found dead (we think he wanted to be an only cat!). After two years ten cats had been killed (one of my sisters was now a veterinary nurse and so had a constant supply of cats nobody wanted). This carnage became too much to bear so we moved again, this time to the country in Chipperfield into a big bungalow with a huge garden and 300 acre field at the back. We had to keep our, by now, eight horses in livery though. Our hand- reared cat named Mole (after the TV character) was killed on the lane just outside the house, after only two weeks and having lived safely in Garston for six years! He must not have realised it was a road as it was so quiet. Thankfully he was the only cat we lost there.

Mole was an incredible character. His mother had been killed on the A405 and left seven kittens which we hand-reared. This is now quite common practice and is quite successful but it was virtually unheard of in those days. There was no special formula for cats and cow's milk was not good for them so many died. We were also unaware at that time that mother cats MUST lick their kittens' stomachs constantly to aid digestion and enable them to go to the toilet and without this it was also fatal. We thankfully found that our German Shepherd Jet absolutely adored the kittens (when she later had puppies she was not a good mother as we think she wanted kittens!). She would lick the kittens and this was far more successful than our attempts with cotton wool. There were also none of the specially designed feeding bottles now on the market so the milk would go down the wrong way. These factors all resulted in four of the kittens dying despite our best, efforts. Mole was to suffer with cat flu which is also common in hand-reared kittens and this left him with one cloudy eye and a permanent snuffle. He loved to sit on people's shoulder as he seemed to find it more comfortable for breathing? Probably he just liked the scream that resulted as he launched himself unannounced on to you. This was to cause consternation to a poor cyclist as we travelled with all of our animals down to our annual holiday on the south coast where we had a second house. We went away for the whole eight weeks of the school holidays as it was then and as the animal population grew we usually ended up having to tow a horse box full of more animals and make a number of journey's to fit everyone in.

Mole hated a cat box so would sit on people's shoulder in the car. At a roundabout he was sitting on the driver's shoulder and a cyclist driving past was so amazed he stared in at the car and lost his footing and thankfully fell inwards on to the roundabout. We had another kitten arrive shortly after named Sylvester and he looked exactly like Mole although without the problems Mole had developed from cat flu as a kitten. He was to get killed two weeks after we arrived in our present house directly outside in the same way as Mole. It was a rather unnerving similarity and he was thankfully one of only two cats to die at Doone Brae Farm on the lane. After three years we found where we live now in Pepperstock where we had a small bungalow but our own land which we had always wanted. The animal population was ever growing and here the horses would be safe from theft although this has been less of a problem since there is no money in horse meat anymore (thank goodness). The cats should have been safe but still in Twenty years four have been killed. It seems nearly impossible to keep them safe unless they are kept in which we don't approve of. We have acquired an ever growing number of animals, as we have never managed to say the NO word. These cover most species, with horses representing a majority. We also have a varied selection of; dogs, cats, pigs, goats, a donkey (a real character who made it to fifty years old), terrapins, pigeons, rabbits, guinea-pigs, chinchillas, chipmunks, budgies, cockatiels, gerbils, mice, hamsters, rats, fish, chickens, ducks, a turkey and even a meerkat found in Dunstable which Whipsenade Zoo agreed to take!

Over the past two years a lot of building work has been completed so that the animals now have a good standard of accommodation and life is easier for myself also! In previous years my mother re-homed many dogs now all the animals who come stay for good.

Chapter II

Cats

Throughout the years we rescued many cats and initially we would try to re-home them where possible. This was more difficult with adult cats as everyone wanted the cute kittens. This was at a time when people allowed cats to continually reproduce and there were many strays around so there were always plenty to choose from. We usually then ended up keeping most of the adult cats. These were many and varied although generally black and white and tabby as they were the most common. My mother loved black cats but they were more rare. We went through a period of time where all the cats were black and white and only one named Tabatha was a tabby and she got very isolated until we took in another tabby called Patrick, his owners wanted him put down because he meowed all the time. He also had a skin condition which left him almost bald but he loved people and would 'talk' to anyone. He particularly liked sitting in the bath probably because it cooled his skin down.

Our first cats after Suzza were Milly and Mandy. They were feral cats no one wanted and we had to keep them in the stable in the back garden for months as we could not get anywhere near them. My mother persevered until finally they would come to her. They came to live in the house and moved on to three houses with us until they died in old age and had become very friendly cats to people they knew.

One of the great cat characters was Flick, she arrived with Tabbatha from a factory where they were over-run with cats and kittens. Thirty kittens and these two cats were caught. They looked after all these kittens between them until we could find all of them homes and they were excellent mothers despite the huge task we were expecting of them. We were happy to keep them afterwards as we were so impressed with their dedication. Flick loved children and each day after school she could be seen sitting on the grass outside our house waiting for the children to come out of school. They would give her their sandwiches and a stroke and we would come out to see a ring of half-eaten sandwiches placed around her.

The most famous of the cats, however, has to be Katie or 'shaky Katie ' as she was known. She had been found on a railway line as a kitten and been brought to the vets. The vets thought she had had meningitis or had suffered an electric shock. They expected her only to live a short while so she came home to live what life she had (actually she had thirteen years of life!) She was not spayed as we worried about the anaesthetic risk and she didn't go out (much) but that didn't stop her producing five litters of gorgeous kittens! Because of her neurological problems she walked with a shaky movement but didn't let that get in the way of normal life. She was a devoted mother and led a very full life.

When we moved to our present house I moved into a mobile home at sixteen and could start taking on my own cats.

These were ones people didn't want and were all wonderful in their own way. Thankfully people in England for the large part began to be more responsible and most cats were neutered so that there were far fewer kittens and feral cats around and as cats and especially kittens became more scarce they became more valued and better cared for although there are certainly still areas were this is not the case.

We did find that when we had around twenty cats at a time they were more accepting of new-comers whereas when we had less it was more difficult to take new ones in, as cats are very independent and if they get upset they have a tendency to walk out!

Chapter III

Electricity!

My father was the archetypal 'jack of all trades, master of none'. We always lived close to the bread line primarily because of the amount of animals we had and so we could not afford to pay people to do odd jobs. It therefore fell to my father to come home from a day's work and be asked to do all manner of odd jobs before he had go out again to another part-time job all in order to pay for the many animals in need we all wanted to help. He got all the best jobs such as unblocking drains, mending stables in the pouring rain and six foot of mud and trying to cobble together electricity supplies when it was totally unsafe to do so. One of my early memories is of one of my sisters flying across the sitting room, quite literally because she had turned a light on my father had 'fixed' and it had given her an electric shock. For my fourth birthday he put up a bedside light on the wall next to my bed and I was so pleased with it that I turned it on and off all night until it blew up, rooting me to the spot and burning two holes in my hand which I have to this day!

As our animal population grew so did the property we lived in until we were in our present farm. We housed the horses in a 300 foot aeroplane hangar and this needed lighting. My father rigged this up and as the roof became more of a hole than a roof over the years rain got onto the wiring and we would try anything to try and ensure the electricity stayed on which would give any Health and Safety inspector a blue fit nowadays. It was as a result of this and the fact that there was a reasonable amount of metal in the hangar that the walls were frequently live so that if you touched them you got a shock, quite literally.

It was on one such occasion when the goats had got into the field next door – which they spent most of their time doing – and we went to try to get them back. They were enormous goats as they had been fed too much as kids and grown abnormally. It was Sammy who was standing by the fence and refusing to come underneath which he could perfectly well do. My sister, myself and one of my sister's friends went to lift him over but every time we got him up on his feet he started to scream and flopped back down. We could not understand what the problem was as goats seem to have a very high pain threshold and we could see nothing to hurt him. We tried a number of times by which stage we were all getting pretty impatient with him. On the final attempt I lost my balance and fell on the wire fence. At this point I realised the problem. A pole was touching the side of the hanger and the fence, it was live with electricity so that each time we lifted Sammy up he touched the wire and got a shock. I got a broom and pushed the pole away and we lifted a relieved Sammy out.

Then there was the day that my sister's mobile home was live. It had never been earthed properly and my sister's husband returned home and went to take the dogs in with him while he went to make the tea. The first dog went in and came flying out passed him again and this happened with the others so he went to put them in again as he thought they were mucking about but again they kept coming back at him like boomerangs. He then touched the walls and realised why when he got an almighty shock.

Years later I had a metal run with boxes in it where the chickens liked to roost and I was cleaning it out with some children helping me. I was inside with two children and the others were outside while we were trying to put it back against the wall. All of a sudden sparks were flying so I shouted for everyone to stand still and we realised that an electric cable was coming out of the brickwork and we had pushed the run up against it. Luckily we all were wearing rubber boots. We were all stuck in there until my father came up to turn the electricity off.

I was also living in a mobile home on the property at the time and my caravan had a distinct lack of earth. I often turned on hot taps at the kitchen sink, as I got in the shower and found that I was washing in hot electricity. My father's defence was always that he no longer felt electric shocks after all these years! When we were finally able to get a qualified electrician in to re-wire the whole place he was horrified by the state of it but I have to say that we never had so many cut outs until it was all made 'safe' and that is very aggravating when you have a lot of animals to look after!

Chapter IV

Horses

I have in total owned 44 horses and one donkey in my life. In all that time, like all of the animals they brought me happiness, fulfilment, reward and financial and emotional devastation! I would not change the time for anything as I have always tried to learn from the bad as well as good in life and of course there are so many stories to tell and all were such characters in their own right.

The donkey's name was Annabell and she lived into her fifties. She had been owned by the owners of the livery stables where we kept our first horses when I was a child. It was years later that we were contacted by her owners who were now in their 70's and in poor health to see if we would take her on. Their options were to take her to a large Sanctuary in Devon which was several hours away and they said they had wanted to keep in touch, or to have her put down. In fact they never visited her, just as most owners do not once their animals are re-homed no matter how good their intentions are! She lived with me for about fifteen eventful years, during which time she essentially did as she pleased, including taking her and her friends off for frequent unaccompanied (by humans) walks!

She died in about the best way possible one spring evening. I had noticed there was something different about her over the previous couple of years but the vet assured me she was fine. Then one morning she wouldn't eat (unheard of for Annabell) and she was off colour, the vet was called and she gave her some antibiotics and painkillers. She said she would be fine but I knew she wouldn't. I kept her in a stable next to her two best friends, they had never been separated in the fifteen years I had owned them all but they seemed to accept it which worried me. They could see each other over the adjoining wall and I checked them throughout the day. At 9.00pm Annabell looked strange but not uncomfortable. When I then checked again half an hour later she was lying dead. I felt badly that I had not been there for her but to be honest I think her friends were of greater importance. I was so worried about Cuddles who had been devoted to her (as I had acquired her as a foal I think she viewed Annabell as her mother and Sooty her other companion as her sister.) As it happened she accepted her death very well and from then on I always let animals see each other once they had died. It was a theory I had previously been opposed to but I am now convinced it helps them to cope far better.

Of course over the years I have learnt so much from all the animals but particularly with the horses I have realised that so much can be healed given sufficient time and patience, both mental and physical ills. Horses in particular suffer as in general people are interested in the job they can do so once they are no longer able to do that job they are lucky to be given the opportunity of survival, the financial and time issues are far more important for horses in consideration of their treatment than say for cats or dogs. In general terms I can say that my horses have lived an average of five years more and with a better quality of life than vets have anticipated. This is not because I am a miracle worker. It is just that I see them as having intrinsic value of themselves and I will always give them the opportunity to 'come right'.

A notable case is that of Monte, he was a 17hh black stunning horse with so much presence that whenever I took him out I would have people stop and stare at him. He had come to me because his loan home no longer wanted him as he had been diagnosed with the breathing condition Chronic Obstructive Pulmonary Disease and so could not work. His owners didn't want him back as he was too costly for them when they could do nothing with him. They then waited a year to contact us and demand money despite the fact that they had asked us to take him and he was worth nothing financially, he also cost a fortune in medical treatment and I could not afford to buy him. As usual however I found the money as I could not part with him. We were advised to call their bluff, knowing full well they didn't want him back! I couldn't take the risk of what could happen to him though and I wanted them out of his life for good. It also taught me a valuable lesson so that all future animals were brought by me for £1 and ownership was signed over.

Monty paired up early on with Fred, a 16hh Thoroughbred who I had acquired because his owner could no longer keep him and his previous owner had wanted him destroyed when he broke his leg for the second time and she could not jump him or claim further insurance pay-outs on him. He is a real character, he loves people and can open ANY door after the practice he gained when he was kept confined for his many and varied leg injuries.

Monty had to have a special mask imported from The States to help with his breathing but it was after I had owned him for a couple of years that a vet doing a routine inspection of the Riding School found it was actually his heart which was the problem. He had a heart murmur. He had been treated for breathing difficulties for years when in fact it was probably his heart which needed treatment. He became quite a celebrity as he suffered two major heart attacks, the second of which resulted in his total retirement. I was thankfully supported by my own vet who said there was no reason why he couldn't have a contented retired life if I did not want him destroyed. He lived for five years after this diagnosis even when I was assured by one vet that he only had half an hour to live! He found adjusting to retired life incredibly difficult initially as it had been such a dramatic cut in his work load so quickly. However once he had appreciated the many benefits such as wandering around loose all day doing exactly as he wanted which included helping himself to the entire haystack now that he had no reason to have restricted access as I was told he had so little time left I let him do as he pleased.

He finally died one summer afternoon. I was working nights at the time so was in bed asleep. The vet was actually at the yard getting her own horse in from the field when she saw Monty walking up the field next to Fred and as they were reaching the gate Monty dropped down dead! Fred was devastated and tried to make Monty stand up, it actually affected him severely and to this day he panics if a horse is ill and goes down in the field. For Monty however I couldn't have wished for better!

Strangely after Monty's death Fred paired up with arch enemy Woody. They hated each other as Fred and Monty had been close since the day they first met and then Woody arrived and also struck a bond with Monty and Fred hated him for it. It was to be of great benefit to Woody though. Woody had arrived because he had tried to kill his owner on a number of occasions. I had not realised this although no doubt I still would have accepted him even though I was very green at the time. He is the only horse I have known who is actually 'dangerous' with really no environmental explanation for it. He had been sent to a dealer for 're-training' before I took him on and was no doubt not treated carefully there but other than those two weeks he really had no bad handling that I could find. He arrived as a three year old and luckily for both of us we have always hit it off well. Two odd bods together!

One of the first indications I had of the problems he had was when he picked up a small child by the head and throw her across the yard. Thankfully she was fine and the mother was very relaxed about it. It was pre the Health and Safety era! I then moved his stable away from passers-by and people were told to stay clear of him. Unfortunately that is like a red rag to a bull to some people who want to prove something! Later on a lady went into the field with him and he came after her, blocked her into a corner and kicked her in the face with the result that he scarred her face and she lost four teeth. Again thankfully she accepted that she shouldn't have gone into the field with him as she had been told not to and she didn't take it out on me! My sister's friend then decided to go and visit him in the stable despite been warned and she got badly bitten on her chest. I put up signs and got very paranoid about people touching him but unfortunately he actually craves attention so he makes my life quite stressful trying to protect him from himself.

In part people were sympathetic to Woody as he had a terrible accident when I had only had him three months. My sister volunteered to go and get the horses in from the field we were renting at the time down the lane. This is not something I was excited about as I prefer to do my animals myself but I was late for an evening course so I agreed. I then heard a panicked screaming after about 15 minutes. I was about to go and check what the –hold-up was and my sister was yelling 'quick we need to get a gun, get a gun quickly'. By this time everyone was shouting at her to get her to calm down and tell us what she talking about. It turned out when she had got to the field she started to get the horses to come in but Monty wouldn't and he was always such a teacher's pet and did everything properly she couldn't understand what the problem could be. She looked around and couldn't see Woody and Monty was running around whinnying and behaving totally out of character. My sister carried on looking and thought Woody must have escaped through the fence and left Monty behind because he was too well-behaved to follow. Then finally as she got near to the other end of the field she could hear some terrible groaning. She thought Woody must have colic or something when to her horror she saw that the owner of the field had dug a trench to lay some piping without informing us and Woody must have tried to jump over it, because that was what Woody was like and he must have slipped on the mound on the other side and fallen in backwards. The trench was the same width as his body so it was as though he had been buried alive. He could not move at all except for his head which he was thrashing backwards and forwards. He had covered himself with earth with his frantic kicking and so could now be barely seen.

I was ordered not to go down to the field as Woody was definitely going to be shot. My sister cannot bear to see animals in pain so tends to look on the bleak side in bad situations. My sister was certain there was absolutely no hope whereas I will fight until I am certain nothing more can be done. I find it increasingly difficult to have animals put down as I get older but I manage to balance this against a sufficient quality of life. My sister was acting with little rationality at this stage and actually went into the nearby gun club and demanded they let her have gun to shoot a horse. They were not surprisingly horrified and as it was illegal they were not about to agree thankfully.

I did go down to see Woody but my sister told me to stay away in case I upset him, my other sister went to sit with him but he kept whinnying and trying to get up. I suddenly realised that the fire brigade may help as they are known to be very good in this type of situation. This was the beginnings of a long standing relationship with them! As these were the days before mobile phones I spent my time running up and down the lane which was not long but it did consist of a virtually vertical hill, with messages for my mother to phone the fire brigade, the vets, hassle the vets to find out where they were; they were stuck on the motorway for hours because of terrible traffic. The whole incident went on for four hours. In total three fire engines came out, we commandeered a JCB from the gun club to help with digging but as the ground was frozen it still took time. There were flood lights put up everywhere. I did sit with Woody in the ditch to keep him calm and we had his head covered to shield him from the earth and the lights.

The vet didn't arrive for hours and each time the firemen moved a bit more earth so that he moved a leg I got a bit more hopeful he would come through although my sister liked to cheer me up with the fact that we didn't know whether he had broken his neck or back yet! Finally we freed the earth and ropes were put around his legs to upright him. As he got up he was totally disorientated by the lights and the fact that he couldn't open his eyes because his head was so swollen from hitting against the sides of the trench and because he had been lying upside down for hours which can be fatal for a horse. He ran straight ahead further into the ditch so that myself and one of my other sisters were throwing ourselves in front of him trying to stop him while the firemen were trying to stop us and shouting at us that we were going to get killed. They threw bales of hay in front of him we had collected earlier thank goodness and he stopped. We then got him to climb up the small bank and stood with him for a while. He just leant on us as if to say OK if you hold me up I can go home now. As we walked up the driveway he gave a whinny and Monty whinnied back, I don't know what they said to each other but they seemed to understand what had happened that night.

Amazingly the worst damage Woody had from the incident was the rope burns on his legs from hoisting him upright. They got quite infected as there was mud etc. in the openings. They eventually healed and the worst one left a mark for a couple of years but you could not find it now. My sister was very worried about vetting him after the incident as she had always been scared of him but it was as if he knew he needed help as he was excellent. It worked in his favour afterwards as people gave him the benefit of the doubt that the accident had damaged his brain even though his behaviour had been erratic before.

There are so many horses to talk about each with such personalities and coming through so much but these are the most notable. Sooty a little black Shetland battled all her life, she had breathing problems, Laminitis in her feet which could get so bad it caused colic mainly because she could take so much pain that she would eat and eat far in excess of what she could manage then finally she battled cancer for four years which I was unaware of until her body was so ravaged she no longer had the strength to get up on her own. This was the time I had to call it a day even though she was still eating, the vet kindly said it was likely that this was no longer a conscious decision but more dementia which was resulting in her displaying manic behaviour. She was put down with an injection, it was only the second time I had it done this way and it was very peaceful and less stressful for me as I hate the gun I just find it the quickest option. Cuddles again coped initially well with the loss as she came to see Sooty's body but then she went into a long period of depression which only really lifted once Henri an abandoned foal from London arrived so that she could share a stable once more which she had done all of her life.

Cossack was the first pony I lost, he was a stubborn bad mannered pony and that kept him going into his thirties and he was brilliant. Dougal had had a terrible life and was terribly neglected. Like Cossack, both grey ponies, he was stubborn and bad mannered. They were both impossible to handle and made life very difficult, Dougal staged a valiant fight although died in his late twenties which was not as old as my average. He had paired with ancient Jack who was hit hard by his death. Baxter was another character but a 17hh Thoroughbred. He had been starved virtually his entire life with the result that he guarded food as though his life depended on it which for most of it it had. I spent the last five years of his life always being terrified to leave him unattended because he would lie down in the field and then couldn't get back up on his own as his knees had been so badly injured during his jumping days that he had bad arthritis. There was the added problem that he didn't like people so I had to get unsuspecting victims to come and help me roll him over until he had enough momentum to get to his feet without them getting their heads kicked in! Luckily our field was on a hill so we could usually get him to roll down with a little help.

Georgie probably deserved a reward for her life. I had her brought for me as a twenty-first birthday present as I had only small ponies and I had cared for my sister's horse for a year while she was in Australia and she had wanted her back on her return which I was devastated about as we had developed a real bond in that time. We went to a large dealer's yard which was a mistake and I fell in love with a gorgeous but very terrified 16.hh Thoroughbred who was too big and powerful for me but primarily too expensive. I still worry what happened to him but that applies to most of the 100+ horses there and the many more across the country. As often happened in my life my mother and sister decide that I should have Georgie who I really didn't want. I could hide my disappointment as I had mouth ulcers so couldn't speak. I felt guilty for not wanting her, she was a lot of money we had never spent that sort of money on a horse before and I did feel sorry for her. The dealer had brought her out cantered her over jumps and she fell and cut all her mouth open so they squirted a hose in it and put her back in her stable. When we next went back it didn't seem as though anything more had been done with her since then.

From the moment I got her home I knew we weren't going to getting along. I wanted the perfect horse (there isn't one by the way) and she was too strong for me I was too inexperienced and it was my sister's horse I loved. The more everyone criticized me because I didn't love her enough the more I resented her. I got her before my birthday and the day after my birthday I took her to a show. I was never a good jumper none of my ponies had liked jumping and my sister's jumping tuition when I was a child had consisted of making me more afraid of her than I was of the jump resulting in me being afraid of everything to do with jumping. Georgie jumped wonderfully but it was only ever at a hundred miles an hour. I went into this tiny arena and headed for jumps but kept ending up nearly climbing the walls as I couldn't stop. I took her outside and went over the practice jump. I jumped it a couple of times and then went over again, pulled her up too much and she hit the pole which flew in the air and hit me on the head and knocked me out. I remember coming round and feeling that I was falling down her neck and that I could nothing about it. Sure enough I hit the ground and was knocked out again and didn't come round until the ambulance arrived. I then was in and out of consciousness for a while. The doctors thought I had fractured my skull but I hadn't so just spent a night in hospital for concussion.

I was frequently knocked out as a child and often when riding but this incident did unnerve me as I was older and I was quite nervous of Georgie, she was probably getting more food and less exercise than she had in her life! We rubbed along together but to be honest we got closer as she developed more health problems and could be ridden less and less. I learnt so much from her however to help with later difficult horses. She went through so many problems in her life. One of my sister's rode her without permission when I had had her about a year and fractured her jaw as Georgie had a delicate mouth and my sister unintentionally has hard hands so she fought with her strength with the result that Georgie threw her head and hit it on the arena wall and lost a tooth and we were later to find out had also fractured her jaw. She had to go to the veterinary hospital for surgery where they all fell in love with her as she was such a wonderful patient as she would put up with anything. She got very phobic about her mouth after this incident not surprisingly and it took years for her to accept medication with a syringe but apart from that you could do anything to her with no complaints.

Georgie years later came out of her stable and caught herself on the bolt on the door and lacerated her side which needed stitches then the worst was to come with her initial bout of lymphangitis. The vet said that she had never seen such a bad case as it spread from her back leg right up her stomach. She was in pain like I had never seen before and for her that was bad. This never left her, once she got over this bout it recurred throughout her remaining ten years of life and was to be what killed her. I tried everything but with the many health issues which had affected her throughout life it seemed likely that she had an underlying lymphatic condition from the start. She was the bravest, sweetest horse I knew and she gave so much I owe her a lot and hope she understood by the end that I had a lot of growing up to do and that I did truly love her. She was one of those animals who made the best of life and it was only in the last year of life that any of her difficulties were starting to grind her down, thankfully she wasn't much affected by pain other horses wouldn't have coped with so until this final year she always looked really good even when she began to blind it didn't affect her she just used Corrie (her best friend) for support.

I couldn't not mention Ginger and Shamus my first two horses as they taught me the most about life and they helped me to get through my many growing pains. Ginger threw me off virtually every weekend as a child and I was invariably concussed for a while. He taught me to fall better! Shamus threw me off a reasonable amount and taught me to hold on to my horse whenever I fell as otherwise he ran off and it would take hours to catch him! He had had a very bad start in life and he was a nightmare in most aspects of life. Initially I couldn't get near him as he would try to kill me. Ginger on the other hand loved people and was very gentle and kind, apart from if I was riding and trying to stay on him!

All I can say is that they were marvellously awful ponies who both taught me that perfection is not the most important thing in life. Shamus was killed in a road accident and Ginger and I were both devastated. Ginger died a year later of liver failure. I went through nearly the first twenty seven years of my life with them and they shared more of my life so far than any other living thing. I went to shows with them and they embarrassed me every time. I only ever paid attention to the first two jumps as I knew I would never get further and I didn't until I rode horses later on and I then found it difficult to remember a whole course. I would have to have someone take Shamus round the show ring so that he was on the other side of the jump to Ginger and myself and then Ginger would jump so that he could get back to Shamus. People would ask to buy Ginger and Shamus when they saw them jumping in the practice ring when they were together and then would be

horrified to see them refuse every jump in the ring. They
taught me humility like no one else could.

Chapter V

Escaping Horses

As with the electricity situation we also never had the money to adequately fence our fields for the horses. This is of course irresponsible but we did the best we could with baling twine and any materials we could find. Someone once joked that the place was held together with baling twine! As a result of this throughout our lives we had the worry and hard work of collecting errant horses from the environs. I remember coming home from school on the school bus and frequently hearing the cries of children that there were horses by the side of the road. They were always ours! I would scream at the bus driver that I had to get off and my brother would run home to get my sisters while I stayed with the horses and tried to ensure they didn't wander on to the dual carriage- way. In general they had no intention of doing so they just wanted the grass on the verge and to come back to the house where they knew they received sugar lumps.

Once we moved to our present farm we had the most frequent escapes. Generally they would do it before school in the morning as they were changing fields or when they got bored in the night so that we would get phone calls from local people that they were in their gardens or were just walking passed their house. I was always late for school anyway but I used to have to explain my reasons each day until the teachers got bored and would just say OK Tamara what is it today dogs, horses, cats or rabbits that caused the problem? The worst times were when all the horses would follow each other and get up a real speed. Particularly when it was rush hour and they were haring around blind bends in the lane. As I couldn't drive my sister would go after them with me in the car and then I would jump out as we got close and run in amongst them to try to get to the lead horse and stop it, or we would drive the opposite way around and head them off and try and stop them. Amazingly I didn't ever get trampled.

My two Shetland Ponies and Donkey were the worst offenders as they were very bright and mischievous, the worst mixture to have! They found any hole however small and went on not so little jaunts all over the place. I would go and collect them with one headcollar and people would be amazed as whenever we had to go out and get the horses there were only a few of us and loads of them so you could only take a few but as a herd the others always followed.

There was one memorable Christmas which had to be the worst case as we had all planned to go out ice- skating. We went to get the horses in and we were trying to rush so we didn't take head-collars but decided to let them come up the road and go in the drive with just us directing them. A very stupid thing to do. Anyway at the junction they decided not to come home but to turn in the opposite direction towards the main road. There was a mile of road before they would hit tragedy and it had been snowing and the conditions were bad. My mother got her car and I jumped in with her. We got near to them but they were taking up so much road we couldn't get passed so I jumped out to get in amongst them but they were going so fast I couldn't keep up. I got in the car again just as we were going to hit the road. The disaster was rushing through my mind, the horses getting killed and them causing a terrible road accident as well. The minutes went on for hours. Then at the last moment the lead horse took a sharp right hand turn and went up a country lane just before the dual- carriage way. I have never felt so relieved up until this day. I got out and stood with them while my mother went to get my sisters to help bring them back as we weren't going to risk another near-miss. I stood quietly while they were standing in someone's garden. The owners came out and tried to shoo them away. I was so embarrassed that I didn't dare tell them what had happened but hid in the bushes trying to stop them spooking the horses until help arrived. We got the horses all back safely. I didn't go ice-skating as I was feeling too ill by this stage.

Chapter VI

Foals

We opened up the local paper one week and saw advertised on the front cover that eleven foals had been dumped in a field just down the road from where we lived. We had actually noticed them a couple of days earlier and had wondered where they had come from. The owners of the field were appealing for any information as to where they may have come from. The article stated that their future was uncertain if the owner could not be found. There was a contact number so I rang up to find out the situation. I was informed that the foals were to be auctioned the next week as it was a legal requirement if ownership could not be established.

I knew it was a bad idea but I decided that I would take the day off to attend the auction and make sure that they found reasonable homes. My father's last words were "don't bother to bring any home!" My mother and I agreed although I had already checked with a local man that he could transport them home if we ended up buying any as we had no trailer! We turned up at the auction and were relieved to see quite a few people there. These poor terrified, bedraggled foals were penned in a circular enclosure with everyone standing around the edge looking at them. There was plenty of grass in the field and they had water but they were clearly very young, they still had curly tails! They had obviously not been handled and looked as though they may be Dartmoor wild ponies. It was the right time of year for them to have come from the Dartmoor sales where poor young souls are dragged from their mothers, usually when they are far too young. They are then taken to market, either sold to the meat man and then end up at a slaughterhouse in England (if they are lucky) or are transported half way across the country and then shipped over to Northern Ireland and then transported down to Southern Ireland, from where they can be shipped to Europe. The English object to the Europeans eating horses so they are not allowed to be shipped straight there alive. Instead their journey is made far more gruelling for the sake of hypocrisy.

From people we spoke to at the auction it seemed that a worker of the owner of the field had felt badly treated and so in retaliation had brought these foals at market and dumped them in the field as he knew that this would cause a lot of aggravation. If this was the case these foals had been brought from Devon on an eight hour trip up to Hertfordshire and dumped in a field with no shelter in the middle of November in the pouring rain when they had only just been taken traumatically from their mothers.

The auction began and they all huddled together as far away from the crowd as possible. The auctioneers were not rough with them but were making them move around so that people could see them and they were getting increasingly frightened. It soon became obvious that most of the crowd had come to watch rather than with an intention to buy. There was a local dealer with a dubious reputation who said she was buying three as she had homes for them. I was not happy but she was quite experience and if she had homes for them they at least wouldn't stay with her for long. There was another lady who wanted one. Everyone tried to convince her to take two as no foals should be kept on their own. She was a typical 'know-it-all type' and there was no getting through to her. That still left seven. I had seen a particularly cute one with a star on his face and so I had decided I would bid for him as I was obviously going to end up with at least two! I brought him for 50p. The highest price that day was £5 from the lady who had chosen the one she particularly wanted, the dealer paid £2 for each of hers and I was left with the rest. They cost 50p each and the sixth and seventh were 25p each!! This was the value of these young creatures but that doesn't stop more being bred each year to have a short life of hell.

The next issue was to get all these very tired babies loaded to travel to their different destinations. The dealer got her three off and I had to wait for my transport to arrive. The plan was to load all the remaining foals on and then get the one who was to go on his own out! There were a group of quite elderly men who were organising the procedure which scared me to death particularly when a man in his sixties was knocked to floor and had to be dragged out of the way of being trampled. Apart from that incident however, the procedure went quite smoothly and the foals didn't get too distressed until the lone one had to be separated which was awful as he was so upset at being taken off on his own. There was nothing anyone could do to persuade this stupid woman so we shut the door on all mine and travelled the few miles home with them all loose which was the safest way.

We arrived back at the farm with nothing prepared as I had hoped that would prevent me from bringing anything home with me! We sealed off the corridor up to the stable they were to go in to ensure they didn't run off and get injured and then opened the back of the lorry. Of course all these foals wanted was to be left alone and they huddled at the back of the lorry and refused to come out. The driver went in to coax them out while I went up to the stable to stop them over-shooting it. They ran up the corridor and straight into the stable, no problem. If they had been children you could have imagined them with bulging eyes at Christmas looking at their presents as their stable was full of dry, deep, clean, warm straw. There was plenty of hay for them to eat and they happily drank straight away from the automatic waterers. I had been concerned as it had taken my horses ages to work them out and thought some wild ponies used to drinking from streams would find them confusing. These proved to be very bright little chaps.

I left them alone for a while to settle in and when I returned found them lying in a heap on the floor on top of one another like a load of dogs. I was amazed as I had never seen horses do this before. There were too many for one stable really as it was certainly a tight fit. They had had enough upset in their short lives however so I decided to leave them together particularly as even if they were split into two groups they were really unhappy. After a few weeks I managed to put them into two stables where they could see each other over the dividing wall. Once they got bigger though they would jump backwards and forwards over the wall even though it was three foot and bigger than they were!

I was like a mother with her first child for the first few weeks as I had no experience of horses this young before. I was on the phone all the time to different people asking every question I could think of. They seemed to sleep all the time. They were obviously so tired after all the stress they had endured and only now having the opportunity to lie in a comfy bed they were taking full advantage of it. Even when I came up and looked over the door they didn't stir so they were getting quite settled but I kept worrying and checking if they were breathing! I later found out they are susceptible to mercury poisoning under situations of such stress so I would have really panicked had I known that at the time.

They got quite used to their routine and each morning and evening before and after work I let them out while I cleaned out a very dirty stable, having so many ponies in it and then later on two. Mostly they ran out and stood at the far end of the corridor while I was cleaning and then ran in once I had finished. After only a few days one of the roans, named Morris would follow me around and look at what I was up to, then the only chestnut one would do it. I named him Folly (my father said one had to be called Folly as recognition of our folly!) I had wanted him particularly as he reminded me of my first pony Ginger and I had always liked chestnuts, he was the second one I chose after Mervin, with the star on his face. Mervin turned out to be one of the biggest characters. Once he decided I was not frightening he didn't bother with the others when I let them out and just followed me around and watched at the stable door while I cleaned it out. If he had been my only one I would have thought I was the second Monty Roberts as he just tamed himself. From very early on he broke away from the other foals and became a close friend of Jack, my oldest pony at 45+. He just loved people, whatever different experiences he had had from the others it held him in good stead.

Of course at only a few months old there was a lot to happen in their lives. They all became very distinct personalities and gave a lot of pleasure and worry which hopefully will continue for a long time to come.

Chapter VII
Corrie

Corrie had arrived at the Sanctuary from an owner who said that she could no longer keep him because she had damaged her back and he was too strong for her to ride any more. When they came to speak to me about him they kept saying that he was grossly over-weight and needed some exercise. I was therefore fairly astonished when he arrived and you could see every bone in his body. It made me wonder what they would think a thin horse looked like! When I took him out for his first ride he nearly killed me as he was so strong but I also found that he had terrible breathing problems. I had him checked out by a vet and found that he had Chronic Obstructive Pulmonary Disorder so this made it difficult for him to go on hacks. I fed him up so he was very keen to go but I worried about the strain on his breathing. Luckily I had years previously imported a mask from Canada for another horse of mine, Monty, with the same condition. This was designed so that horses could receive an inhaler much as human asthma sufferers do. I was able to use this for him and he was such an intelligent horse that when he was having difficulty with his breathing I would only have to come up to him with the mask and he would put his head into it to receive his inhaler.

I hadn't had him long before he paired up with my lovely mare Georgie. She often attracted the male horses but Corrie and Georgie became inseparable. It has to be said that Corrie was more besotted than Georgie but as she grew older she had many health problems, one of which being that she was almost blind. She used to rely on Corrie then to guide her around. I could only ride them out together because, despite not being able to see Georgie would still go like the wind which was very dangerous if she was in front and Corrie was the only horse who could stay ahead of her. Corrie in turn hated being left behind. In the field they were stuck like glue and I have never found such loyalty from a horse even though many are very attached to each other. Corrie seemed quite aware that Georgie couldn't see and he would protect her from getting knocked into by the other horses and guide her in at night. If she got confused especially in the mist or fog he would wait with her until I came.

It was one of those occasions when things turned out for the best as I had taken the day off to go to the auction of the foals. Corrie had been having increasing problems with his breathing and in the summer it had been discovered that he had a large lump on his windpipe. A barium meal was carried out and it was decided that the likelihood was that it was a malignant growth. As he was in his thirties and the prognosis was not good, it was decided that no action should be taken. This was heart-breaking particularly as he was such a wonderful horse. He carried on happily for a lot longer than the vets had predicted but on this day when I came home with the foals I noticed him lying down in the field. He was still lying down once I had the foals all settled in and the other horses were beginning to congregate around him as though there was something wrong and Georgie was moving away. This was the biggest indicator of a problem as Corrie would always stay stuck to Georgie no matter what

It was a horrible November evening as it was cold and damp. I went out to see him and he just lifted his head but remained lying down. I knew this was the end. Fred was getting very agitated, he had been walking with Monte years earlier when he had dropped down with a heart attack and since then he got alarmed whenever one of the horses was ill. Jack likewise gets upset when the others are ill; I don't know whether he senses this being so old himself. I sat down on the damp mud with him and he just put his head in my lap as if to say good-bye. I got someone to bring blankets out to wrap him up over his rug which was difficult as he was 16.3hh! I called the knacker man to come to put him down but they couldn't get there for two hours. I sat with him and the other horses stood around as if to say their farewells and then finally the knacker man arrived. Just at that moment Corrie sensed that Georgie was moving off up the field to go in and he jumped to his feet and ran off up the field after her. I ran after him and let him into his stable just as the knacker men got there. He was whinnying desperately for Georgie but the knacker men thought it was because he was in pain. As soon as I got Georgie they insisted in going in the stable together. By this stage I had changed my mind and was pleading with the knacker men not to put him down that evening. They argued that I was wrong as they could see him wobbling but I could not bear to take him away from Georgie.

Thankfully the men refused to leave as they said he would go down again and I went to get him some food. I knew that if he wouldn't eat then that would be the end as he had been the greediest horse I had ever owned probably because he had been starved for a large part of his life. Sure enough when I arrived with his food he whinnied for it but then wouldn't eat and then he fell to the floor again. I agreed that he needed to be put down and it was a difficult situation as Georgie was in the stable with him and now couldn't get passed him as he had fallen in the doorway. She luckily couldn't see what was happening but the noise of the gun was distressing for her. I wouldn't have them drag him out before he was dead and I didn't want him upset by being separated from Georgie anyway. I let Georgie sniff him for a while before he was removed and actually she missed him less as a person and more because she had relied on him so heavily. She never really quite got over living without him.

The vet had asked if she could do a post- mortem because he had lived so much longer than expected with the growth he had. She was to be even more amazed when she looked at him because the cancer had spread throughout his body and into his spine which is what had made him wobbly and finally unable to stand. She could not believe that he had been so happy, pain-free and full of life for so long. Added to this she found that he had had a broken back as a young horse which had clearly been allowed to heal without treatment. That horse had gone through so much yet was still so lovely!!

Chapter VIII

France

The time has come to consider re-location. I have many issues with England as a country, politically, socially etc. but in the main the house prices are so extreme that the idea of ever obtaining suitable accommodation in order to continue the work I want with animals is impossible. It was for this reason that I began to consider France as an option as the house prices are so much more reasonable despite the influx of English people going out there and pushing the prices up. This would mean that I could afford much more land for the grazing animals which would improve their standard of life and cut down on feed costs and the time it takes when the horses have to be kept in stables at night for the majority of the year because of our lack of land and also because of our awful weather which is far better in the south of France. My dream is to set up a residential centre for people to come and learn about animal welfare and care and to be able to do more rescue work particularly from Spain where the situation is quite terrible in many areas.

The hunt was on. Helped by the cheap flights flying regularly from Local airports it was quite possible to fly often for a couple of days to France to look at suitable places. I searched the internet and looked in magazines. For the most part very little was suitable. The English in general were looking for houses to reconstruct into gites and set up Bed and Breakfasts. I wanted land and lots of it and plenty of out buildings for the animals and a habitable house. I then came across a suitable sounding property so booked to visit. I was met at the airport by a helpful English man who had moved out four months earlier and was helping a local estate agent. I was shown a number of properties, none of which were really what I wanted. The one I went to look at was more run down than I had anticipated and had a 'room' rather than a gite in the middle of the stable yard. There were very close neighbours and the whole of the area near to Burgerac was not really for me. I saw a fantastic Periegion house over a hundred years old and kept immaculately by an elderly man before he died. It actually looked as though he had just left for work that morning. When we entered it was pitch dark as all the shutters were closed but once they were opened a wonderful interior was revealed with lovely antique furniture. Sadly most of the land was wooded; there was no fencing and only limited animal housing; there was an attached neighbour and very noisy neighbours across the lane.

My next visit was through a recommendation and my mother visited with me. We drove into the late evening from the airport in a hire car and I was quite impressed that I managed directions (which I am terrible at in England!) and driving on the right. We had problems finding a hotel but finally stopped at an English run one which was the only one open in the evening. It actually meant we were nearer to our morning pick up point. This was slightly further north than previously and the area was much nicer. The village of La

Coquille where we met the estate agent was beautiful. The house we went out to see was sold before we got there although months later it came back on the market again. We went instead to a property ran as a bison farm and a gite business but the couple had split up and wanted to sell. It was fantastic. There was a small swimming pool Bison proof fencing! I was concerned there were some Bison in the fields still but was told they were already sold. The house inside was wonderfully decorated and the area was so peaceful. We later planned to go back out to put a deposit on the place but were told it was sold. It then, too, came back on the market but by this time my plans were in pieces.

After the Bison farm we had five other properties to look at. Our expectations had been elevated by what we had so far seen and my mother had already been convinced that the Bison farm was the one to buy. The next property was an apple farm, it was very spread out and had a close neighbour. There was actually a lot of potential there but the place was a bit of a nightmare. The owner used cheap east European labour to pick the apples and in both houses there were no facilities other than one toilet and all the rooms were just stacked high full of mattresses and some lockers. It was a very sad place. It would be hard to imagine for a Westerner how you could be that desperate to accept such living conditions even if 'only' for a few months. My mother was horrified and refused to see past the mattresses.

The next property was owned by a nice couple with a dog like one of my mother's and that was enough for her that was all she was interested in after that. It however had a close neighbour and only a partially built 'gite' and the house itself was very confusing with rooms going off here and there and no order at all. The land was spread out and there was no fencing and a right of way passing through. This is just never practical with so many animals living there and their safety to protect.

The fourth place I had been really excited about as the estate agent had asked if I would consider a dairy farm complete with all the cows. The farmer had built up the herd over decades and was well known throughout France. He would sell the farm cheap to someone who would take on the cows and keep the business and he would help out with his knowledge. It sounded ideal. The estate agent was a German who had bred Arab horses and we had spoken about my plans and my view on animals. I had asked if this was purely a dairy farm and explained that in general I am not happy about farming techniques in England and how cruel especially dairy farming is. He assured me this elderly couple loved their cows but that their children were not interested in taking the farm over.

As we drove down the lane we passed an elderly woman carrying a fairly skinny white cat which we commented on. As we drove through the gate there was an elderly dog lying outside and a younger one straining at a chain and barking, it had a tatty dog kennel but nothing else. My mother commented that she thought this was not going to be 'my sort of a place' how right she was to be!

The lady with the cat was the farmer's wife and she entered the yard with her daughter and son-in-law as we began to look around with her husband. He said to look around outside first and opened the first shed. There were three young cows standing in a small enclosure which had clearly not been mucked out in a long time. They were standing on what was left of dirty, sodden bedding but essentially it was excrement. There was virtually no natural light in the shed once the doors were closed and there was another older calf tethered at the other end of the barn to the wall. They all had rings through their noses.

Because I am nosy I decided to further investigate the shed and to my horror found a very young calf tethered in even more filth than the others round the back completely in the dark with a muzzle on and just pitifully trying to call to me or anyone who would listen. It had big sorrowful eyes I will never forget. In my naivety I thought initially it was ill like horses can be and needed to be muzzled. I came out and asked the estate agent to find out why it was being kept like that. At that moment the penny had already dropped for me. The farmer replied with pride that he was being prepared to eat (this was a calf selected for veal.) Of course I knew this happened, I knew it was legal in France and I knew there was nothing I could do about it. My mother said we could buy it but he probably wouldn't sell it and he would only choose another calf to do the same to. It was better in my view this calf finished its misery and was killed. I have never felt so useless and as though I had so badly let an animal down, I burst into tears.

The estate agent and my mother asked what was wrong and I told them there was a veal calf in there. The estate agent didn't understand what I was talking about so my mother explained and also pointed out that the practice was illegal in England although calves are still sold live abroad and then turned into veal. English hypocrisy at its best! The farmer was completely confused and had no idea why I was so upset. I explained to the estate agent that there was really no point in continuing the viewing as I could never work with people with these views on animals. He was remarkably understanding and said he also disapproved and didn't realise we would come across this situation but that I needed to look around as it would be difficult to explain otherwise.

We looked around but I felt sick to my stomach and so disgusted at myself. We looked around the buildings. The milking parlour was ancient but immaculate but all the barns were six foot in faeces. The house was horrendous. It was very dark like most of the houses but that was a blessing. It wasn't exactly dirty but it hadn't been decorated in a few decades and it was an absolute tip. Their grandchild had a cot in one room and you could barely get to it for all the rubbish around it. It was in short a terrible end to an otherwise exciting day. I had a splitting headache and felt really ill. We left and were all very relieved to do so.

We stopped at a café in the village down the road which was very picturesque but all I could think of was that poor calf I had left behind without helping, the thought stayed with me for months afterwards until I could feel fairly sure it would be dead and out of suffering. We had a cup of tea and then made our way back to where we had left our car. We had instructions of where to eat and stay the night but only managed to find our way back to the same hotel we had stayed at the previous night. They were not serving food as they had had a big festival that day and they were not going to make any special arrangements for us so we made our way to the nearest eatery. We avoided McDonalds etc., and ate at a French fast food restaurant. It was not top cuisine but I found something vegetarian. We were amused to see dogs in the restaurants being given water from bowls by the waitresses. Something you would never see in England!

We were up next morning to meet the estate agent again who was bravely taking us to see another farm. We were all now quite worried about this and the poor man went in first and spoke to the farmer to try and ensure I would be happy with what I saw. This farm was in the usual untidy state of French and probably most farms but nothing terrible. Considering the man lived there alone the house was amazingly tidy. He had a dog tied up outside but there was a bowl and basket in the house and he said it was only tied up while he was busy in case it ran on to the road. He kept apologising that the chickens and ducks were all still shut in but he was running late. Everyone was very worried by this stage that I was going to criticise him. We were worried at one point as we noticed he had some of the ducks which were used to make fois gras. When we questioned him he said he didn't do this as he didn't have time to force feed the birds! The chickens and ducks were all free range, once he let them out in the mornings! We were amazed to see a hen with all her tiny chicks wandering around loose amongst the cats. The farmer said the cats didn't touch them. He also had names for all the cats, which although quite thin seemed perfectly happy. The French cats do seem to have a petite frame but in general they are also not looked after. The tendency is to let them have kittens continually and drown them rather than having the parents neutered.

We walked all over the farmland which was rather untidy but I wasn't allowed to look in the barns where some cows were. The estate agent assured me that there were not any veal calves in there but I think he was too worried by this stage to let me see any more animals in case I was unhappy about their living conditions. The farmer had a gigantic vegetable patch (well field actually) which was immaculately kept. We left the farm to talk about the properties we had seen and my mother from the start had basically decided on the Bison Farm. We were going to see a goat farm on the way back to the airport but we had all chickened out. The estate agent kept explaining to me that all the goats would be inside as it gets too hot for them in the summertime but my mother and I decided not to risk it anyway.

I went back to France a few weeks later as I had found an advert for a farm which was too good to be true. It was an up and running riding holiday centre for the same price as the Bison Farm. It had eight bedrooms with en suite bathrooms and sky TV in each room, stables a lot of land and an indoor swimming pool! I felt I needed to go and check it out before we committed to the Bison Farm.

I was met at the airport by a lady who the owner had asked to pick me up. I was told she wanted the work and also had a B & B. Unfortunately the owner had given neither me nor the lady a name or description of the person to look for. I sat down with my name on a board and another lady was talking to someone at the other end of the arrivals lounge. We were there for quite a while until I overheard her conversation about coming to pick someone up to look at a house. I plucked up the courage to approach her and ask if she was looking for me. We decided that she was and we went to her car.

It was quite a journey to her house and she made me feel rather awkward as she gave me the impression I was rather putting her out. She said she was going out in the evening and was in the middle of decorating and that this was all rather out of the blue. She asked me about my plans and then said she was trying to sell her house so if I didn't like the farm I had come to see I could buy her house. I did keep pointing out that I had really found my dream house. This I was glad about once I saw her house!

We arrived to a very shabby, large house right on a main road. We went in and she unchained the dog. She said she only chained him in case I didn't like dogs but I wasn't very impressed. The dog actually didn't seem to like her much and kept following me around the whole time I was there, but then his owner was very stressful. She said that the dog didn't eat well, which I wasn't surprised about, when she put the bowl down she continually shouted at the dog to eat, not surprisingly he didn't find it a pleasant experience. The owner went out for evening and I sat with the dog. It wasn't a lovely house. The owner told me it had been owned by an old lady who had a lot of animals and hadn't kept it well so it was a total tip when she moved in. That was two years ago but it still looked rather like she had only recently moved in. She had virtually no food in the house and made me feel a little as though I was an inconvenience so it made me smile when I left and she asked me to recommend her to my friends as she was desperate for the income.

The lady I stayed with had forewarned me not to be too excited about the farm we went to see the next day. She had said it was like "Essex come to France". I couldn't help but be excited although I usually find in life that what seems too good to be true is in fact so, this was to be no exception. As we drove in, we initially had to fight with the gate which wouldn't open and then we drove into what had been called the courtyard in the advert. Well it looked as though the owners had suddenly had to leave in a hurry and there were chairs and tables and various other articles strewn about the place. You could see that this had been a lovely old French property and with careful restoration it could have been wonderful again. Unfortunately it had been subject more to vandalism than to restoration. The tiled roofs and been patched with asbestos corrugated sheets, the old brickwork which made up the walls of the barns was patched up with plywood sheets and there was worse to come inside the house. The owner must have had a furniture business as every room had a dirty looking three - piece suite in it. The whole effect was shabby and dirty but what was worse was that the old wooden beams and brickwork walls were ruined with plaster board stuck on which had been badly cut so there were gaping holes and plastic foam squirted in the roof which had dripped down the walls. There were extra rooms made all over the place, many with little or no natural light to them, there were staircases where you had to jump up to get to the upper floor, corridors so it was like a rabbit warren and bathrooms everywhere. There were tiled ones, ones with shell shaped bathroom suites in, shower cubicles stuck in the middle of the room and everywhere you went there was another one. There were two kitchens which had cupboards barely hanging up and looking as though they had been thrown at the walls, then, just for good measure, in one kitchen they were painted with an orange marble effect.

The overall effect of the house was to make you want to cry, all I kept thinking was I hope that no French man ever comes to look at this. The French are obsessed with septic tanks of which there were none to be found so as well as all the health and safety issues, the French authorities would have had a field day. There is no way they would allow this place to be run as a business. They are very strict about regulations and this was a death trap. The last thing to mention was the indoor swimming pool. By this stage I had decided that there was no point in scrambling through the undergrowth down a sheer drop to look at the land which came with it. I shuddered to think how horses had got there safely. All around the outside of the buildings there was broken glass, old bits of wood and abandoned machinery and vehicles. I just wondered what anyone coming for a holiday in a fantastic setting such as this would think!

I plucked up the courage to enquire about the swimming pool and was taken into one of the buildings which looked half fallen down, it was right next door to the one which housed the stables the owner had advertised. These made my amateur attempts at brickwork look impressive as no brick was straight and all the walls leant at different angles like a group of Leaning Towers of Pisa. The swimming pool was a big pond in the middle of a large amount of decking which had been badly laid so that there were gaps in-between. I really had seen enough and felt relieved that this made a clear choice for the Bison Farm!

We had tickets booked to go out and put a deposit down on the Bison Farm which the owner had promised the estate agent he would hold for us (we found out later that he had been trying to sell it for two years!) We then got an email a week before we were due to go out to say it had been sold. The wife of the owner (they were separated) had sold it to someone else. We were devastated and the estate agents advice to buy one of the properties quickly before they went didn't appeal to us.

It was a few weeks later that I saw another advert for another really great sounding place. This time I found the website for the agency with all the details of the property including photos and it really did look as good as it sounded. It was also cheaper than the other properties we had looked at. I flew out that weekend as there were other buyers driving down to look. It was an absolutely gorgeous stud farm.

There were two houses, neither were as nice as the Bison Farm, but they were habitable and just needed some decoration. It was in a nice area and the lanes were very quiet. There was a beautiful lake at the end of the land. People fished there which I wasn't too keen on but it was very pretty. There was also a pond on the farm itself. There were a variety of buildings including stable blocks and massive barns, they had –self-filling water troughs and automatic lighting. The fencing was adequate and there was a lunging area as well as a medical room and buildings for chickens, goats, pigs etc. It was truly fantastic.

There was another place to look at which was nowhere near in the same league but it was substantially cheaper. However, it needed a lot of work and the land was split up all over the place with no fencing and it had been used for crops rather than pasture. The family were very desperate to sell as they had been very badly treated by the French organisation SAFEIR who deal with sales of farms and land. Sadly this was really not what I felt was suitable for me.

I returned to England totally elated and my brother was to go out and look and see what he thought of the place. Unfortunately for me the estate agent had decided that I needed looking out for and that I would not be able to cope on my own and so had been constantly on the phone to my mother telling her I should not buy the place. My brother went out to see the farm as my mother felt that he needed to make the final decision and he was putting the money into the purchase as he wanted to have my inheritance of my mother's farm at home. He decided that I would not be ale to cope and advised my mother against allowing me to go ahead. My mother was having second thoughts about me moving to France at all and was beginning to show cracks. When my brother returned he told my mother she should not let me go. I was devastated! To add insult to injury the Bison Farm AND the original gite complex I had been going out to view on one of my first trips had then come back on the market, so there were now three fantastic places to choose from, but my mother would no longer consider it.

I was now facing a winter in England with all the rain and mud that came with it as well as huge animal feed bills and mounting veterinary bills from various tragedies which had occurred that year. There was the added burden of the rift which had been caused in the family; two of my sisters were very against me going to France. I was unhappy with the way my brother had behaved and my mother felt I was ungrateful and demanding. All was not well. After a few weeks I had picked myself up and decided not to give up. I needed to find a way to pay my debts off, learn French and prepare for a secure future in France where I could have an adequate home for myself and all my animals and financial security. It was not clear at this stage how this would happen as things were looking very bleak but I decided to think positive! Even when things have looked hopeless in the past, if not good at least something positive has at some stage come out of it. Since I was a child being told by teachers I wouldn't pass exams I have proved people wrong so this would just have to be another instance. I didn't know when it would happen. I always work on the assumption, though, that good things are worth waiting for and are all the better for it. This is especially the case if you have had to work particularly for it. Watch this space!

Chapter IX

Dogs

I have owned fewer dogs myself than I have horses but I was also involved with the dogs my mother had re-homed over a period of years. As with the horses all I can say is that they taught me so much and I have no doubt that they made a far better person than I would have been without their input. Of course they cannot work miracles so they could only work with the material available to them!

I looked after some dogs which were re-homed. The first was a Poodle I named Joanna, I had her sleeping with me in my bed and she was just the sort of dog I always wanted, rather than the Rottweilers and Alsatians we had! I took her to her new home, I was terribly upset but she lived to be about sixteen and by all accounts was very happy. I looked after an adorable dog called Pixie but my German Shepherd Rosey hated her and she also found a home. I was less happy about this one but had no say. I then had Kibby. A little mongrel who was devoted to me and surprisingly Rosey was quite content with her but there was a very good home which came up for her and I felt it wrong to deprive her of it. She actually also required a lot of veterinary treatment as a result of a road accident she had suffered as a stray and her new owners were prepared to spend a fortune on her. She also lived to be a good age.

My own dogs started with Scooby a West Highland White Terrier my mother had bred. She was quite a character and her and Rosey were very jealous of each other. Scooby amazingly lived to be a great age considering that she would attack the big dogs who would finally retaliate with disastrous consequences. Scooby was probably the most stitched up dog in history and this had no effect on her desire to antagonise the other dogs.

Rosey and Major, my first Rottweiler like Ginger and Shamus have a lot to be thanked for. I learnt through them and they suffered my mistakes. I was one angry child and teenager – well, if the truth be known – into adulthood, too. I didn't get on with my family; I wasn't popular at school so I was alone in the true sense of the word other than for my animals. This meant that I solely relied on them and thank goodness they were forgiving. I was obsessed with cleanliness but had a very short temper. My first animals taught me so much about the truly important things in life. Now when I am in debt when I am battling with muddy fields and I get caught up with the insignificant things in life I can see that as long as you have those important to you and they have their health and you are doing more good things than harm you can carry on and find a solution to problems.

I have found in general that the dogs rather than bitches are more devoted but essentially animals forgive so much, if you shout and they don't understand they don't hold it against you, if you are crying they are the first to come over and be with you, they look at you as if to say 'let me help'. I love all my animals and couldn't say that I could be without any species but the dogs because they are so close to you seem to know you like no other. If I am honest, I would like my first animals back so that I could do everything better, as well as the fact that I still miss them terribly. It must be like parenting children that you would like practice runs before the real thing.

Major was an excellent dog we gelled straight away and he was so funny. He would come out on horse rides and lie down in front of cars to make them stop, partly because he wanted to get in and have a lift! This is a trick which he passed on to his companions who in turn passed it on although now it is a matter of standing in front of the cars as no dog can be as lazy as Major was! It is this type of behaviour which keeps the memory of animals alive years later. Rosey was a very jealous dog and in hindsight reminded me of myself. She was quite an angry dog and I feel, as was the case in my childhood, she didn't feel loved enough by me as I wasn't really sure how to do this and this I regret. Both lived to an old age but I would like a second chance with them to repay all I learnt from them. As this is not possible I have put this into practice subsequently and can never tell and demonstrate enough to my animals how much I love them.

I took on a Border Collie Gemma and sadly we didn't gel, I couldn't cope with her devotion, she was stuck to me all the time and I needed to have a lot of personal space I found it difficult to demonstrate love and affection, thankfully she was very attached to a local man and she went to live with him where she was very happy. Equally my second Rottweiler Rocky and I didn't get on at all yet he loved my sister so he lived with her but sadly died prematurely of cancer. It hurts me to admit to all of these cases where I feel I failed except that I have always tried in life to learn from mistakes. I had a lot of problems to work through and I couldn't offer these dogs the best but I hope I did the next best.

My next group of dogs benefited from my previous errors, there was Walter who was a Rough Collie who had been badly abused by his previous owners. He was elderly when he came to me, had three legs and was nearly blind but he was excellent. He tried to attack most people but he especially hated my sister which was a little uncalled for as she had actually saved him from being put down at the vets. He used to run after her to bite her and even attacked her car if she was in it! He did however adore me and people would note how his eyes lit up when he saw me.

Into this bracket come Fowler, Sophie and Kira. Fowler was a gorgeous black Labrador he had been first discarded by his owners as he had a recurring stomach complaint and then by a vet who 'rescued' him. He was a fantastic dog but sadly Kira couldn't see this and they fought every day for a year! They settled down and everyone loved Fowler he wasn't a great character just the nearest you could possibly get to a perfect dog. He was killed on the road about a year after Walter when my brother let off fireworks, which admittedly unexpectedly, spooked Fowler who ran off for two miles before being killed instantly. Sophie was a terrible wanderer and she adored Kira and the feeling was mutual. I had to keep my eyes on them every second as they loved nothing more than to go for long walks (between 4 – 8 hours) on their own. They always returned after I had looked for them or called the police or collected them from somewhere (one occasion 5 miles away). My fear was they would get run over and people said I should keep them locked up but I couldn't do that to them. Actually what happened was Sophie was stolen, two years later I still keep searching as there is a terrible problem with dog theft which the police will not accept and certainly will not act on.

Then to the last devastation which was Kira's death, he was like a child with learning difficulties. He was so loving but obsessive, he never got over Sophie leaving but he also never could be dissuaded from annoying the neighbouring dogs to the extent that in his final year I could not keep him in the house if I was not there. He would escape through any window left open for the cats. I went for a job interview in London and was only gone two hours. I had a frantic phone call to say Kira had escaped and had been pulled through the fence by the neighbour's dogs who had inflicted terrible damage to him. The vet was going out to collect him and bring him back for surgery. It took me what seemed like forever to get back from London and Kira was just being operated on so I couldn't see him. He was operated on for four hours and for two hours afterwards it was touch and go as his heart had stopped during surgery. I really thought he may pull through as although he was old he was quite determined but it wasn't to be. I don't know what went through his mind the vet said he didn't seem to suffer at all but it was another case where I felt I had let an animal down by not being there to protect them. All I can say is that contrary to many people's belief that if you have a lot of animals you can cope better with loss you don't. I have only been that desolate on a few occasions and I find it like a physical pain every time an avoidable catastrophe happens.

Chapter X

Jake

I had a phone call one summer afternoon. The lady had seen
my newly launched website (the idea was to raise money to
enable me to finance all the animals I already had, in fact it
was attracting more!) She asked me if I would take in her
young male Rottweiler, she had a pub in Kensington in
London but had to return to Australia unexpectedly. She had
no one to take the dog and she didn't want him to go into
kennels. I said she could bring him up and see how she got on
with my animals. She didn't sound very sure about his
temperament with other animals and said he was a problem
with other male dogs on a lead. I did explain that virtually all
dogs are aggressive towards other males when on a lead. It was
arranged she would bring him up at the weekend. She arrived
late as she had lost her way. She then got him out of the car on
a lead whereby he nearly pulled her over. I said I would walk
him up as I was worried about all my free range chickens. In
fact I had never seen such a placid dog once he was allowed to
walk up the drive. He had seen very few other animals in his
life, it turned out that he had spent most of his two years shut
in the flat above the pub so just about everything was new to

him. Despite this he took everything in his stride and barely noticed the birds or cats.

I decided to introduce him to my dogs in the field and told the owner to let him off the lead and start walking across the field while I let my dogs out, Kira a Samoyed and Eddie another male Rottweiler. To my horror as I came out she still had him on the lead and he was jumping six foot in the air and getting very excited. I shouted to let him off and she kept saying that she didn't think she should. Finally she did as I requested and once he was let off he flew up to my dogs, hackles raised, they all walked around each other and then ran off playing. I tried once more to explain that dog's instinct is to protect their owner when on a lead and so they will show aggression to other dogs, particularly male ones but she didn't seem to understand. We walked through all the horses in the field and again Jake showed no interest. He was more interested in their droppings on the field.

Everything was fine and then the owner suggested she take him back home and bring him back the following week as the vet had suggested that would be less upsetting to the dog. I didn't agree but said she could do that if she wished. In my experience dogs rarely miss their owners if they are in a pleasant environment even if they are very attached to them. In this case actually I was wrong. When she returned with Jake the next week, we unloaded all his belongings and she said a tearful and protracted good-bye. I assured her he would be fine and walked away from her with him while she drove off. He then gave me a terrible shock as I let go of him he took me completely by surprise and ran off after her. I ran to catch him and thankfully on the drive we had a red car parked and he thought it was his owner's red car so was desperately trying to get into it. I caught hold of him and brought him back but he was very unsettled. I let him get into my car where he seemed to feel more secure. Of course for a dog who had barely seen the outside of the same four walls in his life it must have just been too much to take in. For nearly two weeks afterwards he really just wanted to stay in the car whenever he could. He was a very sorry figure. He was scared of his own shadow.

Jake began to settle in and although he found the horses worrying he was absolutely fine with all the animals which was very fortunate. His life took a definite up turn when Spotty arrived. I was very worried as Spotty is a very small Jack Russell who is entire and had a very bad start having been beaten and starved. I didn't know how all the dogs would settle, mine being so much bigger. As always they were excellent and accepted him brilliantly. Spotty and Jake however became firm friends almost straight away and this developed into an inseparable relationship whereby Spotty could and did do anything he wanted to Jake.

Everything was looking very good and Jake was settling in well, he had a superb temperament and I had no concerns about him at all. Little did I know that he and I were to have the most horrendous eighteen months possible. My eldest sister had run a riding school for years and unlike me she loved having loads of people around her. She loved chaos and disorganisation and attracted people like a magnet, both adults and children. Many of the children stayed over the weekends and holidays and often in the evenings. They tended to have fairly dysfunctional families and often spent the night either in the barns or with the horses. One of these children who had spent years coming up as a child when she had little home life had suddenly turned up again, now in her twenties and with a child in tow. My sister had by now moved away and in my short career as a teacher I had actually taught her and so I got stuck with her. She was never really very interested in the animals she had begun coming up with other girls who were very keen on horses and as she had so little in her life she had continued to come up for the social setting rather than because of the animals.

Her life had never looked very promising, she had left school with no qualifications. She had been very unpopular with all the teaching staff there, primarily because her elder sister and brother had been continually in trouble and she had done nothing to break the mould. She had no family support and had never made any effort academically. She had surprisingly done an equine course at college after school which she didn't finish but did go on a trip to New Zealand as a result. She didn't intend to go into an equine field as she realised that it wasn't for her. She was fairly wary of all animals including horses; she was very lazy and really wasn't interested and didn't understand animals anyway. Luckily for her she managed to get pregnant straight away while only eighteen anyway so her problems were solved. She blamed the doctor, as everything in her life was always someone else's fault. This entitled her to a free house and ample money to live on in benefits with certainly no need to work. She could move out from living with her mother and as her mother really liked babies she was also a free babysitting service.

I cannot say that I was overly keen to have mother and child visiting. The mother couldn't do anything with the animals and was unreliable and she essentially wanted herself and her daughter to ride the horses at no cost. I felt quite sorry for her as she was obviously lonely. She went through a whole list of why her life was a mess which was as I was about to find out the typical story of it being down to everyone else and taking no responsibility herself. She seemed to have a lot of difficulties. She was in a council flat which she desperately wanted to move out of as she said no one liked her and that her neighbour was mad and making her life hell. She continually talked about how she wanted some money to put down on a house so she could move away. She wanted to stop contact between her daughter and her –ex-boyfriend because she said he was a 'waste of space' and holding her back and she was reliant on her mother and her mother's boyfriend to look after her daughter. I said that I thought she was wrong to stop her daughter seeing her father as she was really attached to him. I was also struck by the fact that the first time her daughter came to visit and spoke she just kept saying to Kate 'mummy look after me and don't let anything happen to me, mummy you have to look after me'. I questioned the mother about this as I thought it was unusual that a child would keep saying this and the mother said oh yes she doesn't trust me as I keep letting things happen to her. I was quite shocked.

The first time the mother had asked if her daughter could have a free ride on the ponies I said she would have to lead her as I was leading another little girl. She put her on the pony and then walked off and left her while she went to the car to get a drink. Luckily another mother caught the pony and although her daughter fell off she didn't badly hurt herself but I was cross and Kate just said oh well she has to learn how to ride. I tried to explain that you MUST stay with a small child ALL the time but it didn't seem to get through. On another occasion she put the child on a pony without permission and left her, when I said that was irresponsible she replied oh he's so old he wouldn't have done anything. On a further occasion she completely lost the child at the farm and hadn't even noticed until it was pointed out and I went off to find her. She was crying and said her mummy had left her. She also used to leave the child strapped in a pushchair with a male turkey I had at the time and couldn't understand that there could have been the possibility of the turkey pecking the child.

Unfortunately without being nasty it was impossible to deter her from coming up. My father was diagnosed with terminal cancer and then died unexpectedly quickly. He had never liked this girl which was strange as you could count the people on one hand he didn't like. We had put it down to him being bad tempered because of his illness. If only we had listened! The week after he died we had a heat-wave, I was feeling very low and I decided that I would take all of the dogs down to the coast where we used to own a holiday house. It was a place we had spent a lot of time in our childhood and my father had loved the place. I had mentioned this and the young girl had asked if she could come and bring her daughter. I knew she did not love dogs so I warned her that I was taking all of the dogs, she said that was fine and she really wanted to go out for the day. Without being horrible I didn't see how I could get out of it. I told her I wanted to leave really early in the morning and still she wasn't put off.

In hindsight the whole plan was not such a good idea. It was the hottest day of the year so I thought that no one would be stupid enough to drive anywhere (except for me). Unfortunately I was wrong and the roads were jammed pack the whole way. As usual, as I am not known for my punctuality we had left later than intended and instead of the two hours it should have taken it ended up taking four hours all in all. The car had no air-conditioning, the child was getting fed up and was crying and the mother was putting hats etc. on the dogs. I tried to get through to her that when the dogs were all boiling hot this was really not a good thing to do but I might as well have been talking to a brick wall. As we got near to the beach, the child was really getting restless so I explained that we would be at the sea soon. This only made matters worse as she was then screaming. Her mother then brightly said that her daughter hated the beach. This was only one further sign of her lack of consideration for her child. I asked why she had asked to come if the child hated the beach and her reply was simply that she had wanted to come so it was tough. At this stage there was little I could do. I had intended to go to the beach and drop the mother and child at the park for the day.

When we reached where we had owned our house I parked the car outside a friend of my parent's house. I got all the dogs out of the car and put them all on leads. I held the two Rottweilers and the Samoyed and the mother insisted that she and her daughter held the two Jack Russells. We went on to the beach only to find that dogs were no longer allowed on them. We then walked with all of the dogs about a mile up to the private beaches at the end of the promenade where dogs were allowed and all the dogs had a drink from some bowls a lady leaves outside her house for dogs. The two Jack Russells and Samoyed were let off their leads and the two Rottweilers remained on leads while we walked down the beach. I went ahead of the mother and daughter and took both the Rottweilers in the sea with me still on leads.

There were other families on the beach so I chose an empty spot in order that the dogs didn't splash anyone. I kept the dogs on the lead until we were a good distance out from the shore and then let them off and played with them in the sea and let them swim for a few minutes. I then put them back on the lead as I walked back to the shore.

When I got back to the shore the mother was still a way up the beach. I called out that I thought we should move further back up the beach because I had cut my feet and legs on the barnacles on the stones which were horrendously sharp at that particular spot. The daughter was in the water on her own which concerned me and the mother said to leave her there as she was happy so I walked back with the dogs to be nearer to the daughter in case anything happened in the water. As I was watching the daughter I realised that I had the dogs on the wrong leads. I wanted to swap them over so I took Jake's lead off momentarily and as I went to put the other lead back on, the daughter started playing in the sea and screaming with excitement. At that moment Jake turned and ran up to her to play and jumped up at her and knocked her over. He landed on top of her as she fell on the floor and I ran over and shouted at him and put him back on the lead. The mother was out of vision initially as she was a way away and she then ran up and picked the daughter up and cuddled her.

A man on the beach was walking towards us and saw the whole thing. He walked past unperturbed and as we were going up the beach to make sure the daughter was alright he called me back to tell me that I had dropped one of the leads. He then said to me "it is a shame when that happens isn't it" and walked off very unconcerned. The other families on the beach had also seen what had happen and no one came over in a panic at all to see what had happened.

I had all the dogs on leads as we walked up the beach and a lady from one of the houses along the front said that I could put all the dogs in her house while I went to check if the daughter was OK. The lady in question is in her eighties and has problems with her knees making mobility difficult. She looked after all five dogs which she had never met before for two hours in a one-roomed house and said she felt totally unconcerned about their temperaments.

When I got back to the mother she was holding the daughter but hadn't checked if she was hurt so I told her to take her top off to check her over. She had scratches on her legs which were as a result of the very sharp stones and she had marks on her shoulder where Jake had contacted with his teeth as he fell on her but the skin was not broken it was just bruised. There were no rips or tears to her clothing at all. The worst injury was on her front where she had fallen on the stones and of course Jake being a heavy dog and falling on her had increased the pressure of very sharp stones on delicate skin. This was, of course, a distressing injury for all concerned.

I stayed with the mother and daughter while we waited for the ambulance. I was very upset that the day had been ruined for everyone and Kate said that she accepted that it was just an unfortunate accident and that the dog was in no way to blame and in fact said that she felt responsible as she should have been looking after her daughter. She said she certainly didn't want the dog punished for a complete accident when she knew that he had a good temperament. I said that there were mistakes on both sides and I volunteered that I would not allow Jake out with young children in future.

It seemed to take a very long time for the ambulance to arrive. Initially a paramedic on a motorbike arrived and took a look at the daughter and said that it wasn't very serious. Two men in an ambulance then arrived and had no bandages with them and took a long time to dress the wound caused by the stones. They also didn't seem too concerned. I said I was worried in case the daughter had hit her head or if she was shocked but they seemed very laid back and calm and couldn't work the blood pressure monitor so left it and then took the daughter and mother off to the hospital. I went back to get all the dogs and take them back to the car and back home. I stopped at the hospital on the way as I couldn't get hold of the mother and I was worried about her daughter but I couldn't find anywhere to park and it was too hot to leave the dogs in the car even in the shade. I drove off and waited in the car until I heard from Kate who said that everything was OK and that the daughter was not badly hurt. She said that the doctors didn't want to stitch the cut made by the stones because they were not sure if it was a dog bite or not. I explained that I was certain it wasn't because Jake just fell on the daughter from behind and the cut was on her front and with no marks to her clothing he couldn't have been responsible. She said she would tell them but I gather they continued to delay stitching it because they said an expert would have to look at it and it was finally stitched a number of days later when she was moved to a different hospital.

The injury was fairly minor but ANY bite from human or animal can get infected so particularly with a small child doctors do of course need to take precautions and more importantly as she had been knocked out she needed to be observed. The main issue however, as I later found out, was that social services were already involved with the family due to concerns over the care of the child and the capability of the mother to properly provide for her.

For the first week we spoke every day on the phone (Kate rang me as well as me ringing her) as I was concerned about the child. The mother said each time that the child was absolutely fine and kept asking when she could come and see me and the dogs. I offered to take her car back to her house so she didn't have to come up and she declined saying she wanted to come and see me and the animals with the child. She also phoned my sister up until the day before I was arrested asking when she could go up and see her and her animals (she has six very large dogs), she told her she had not wanted the matter to go further but had been forced into it. I have also been told that she expects to receive a large amount of compensation which, is why she says she is doing it.

She told me that the police and nurses had put pressure on her to make a complaint and that she had not wanted to, that she DEFINITELY DID NOT want the dog put down for a pure accident and that the police had blackmailed her by telling her that they would place the child on the 'At Risk' register if she refused to co-operate. Her nieces and nephew had all recently been taken into care and the family were allowed no contact with them so she said that she was scared. She phoned my sister the night before I was arrested to say that she felt terrible because her mother, the father of the child and the mother's boyfriend were all forcing her to make a complaint when she didn't want to.

After the incident the mother immediately said, " Oh God my mum's boyfriend and my –ex-boyfriend hate dogs and told me not to let the child anywhere near them". Later when the mother's own mother and her boyfriend came up to collect their car the boyfriend kept saying these dogs shouldn't be allowed they shouldn't be out in public places. When people I know have seen the mother or her mother out they have virtually crawled along the ground and won't look them in the eye which doesn't not strike me as someone with a clear conscience.

I was to find out why they all looked so uncomfortable a week later when I was called on by the local police and asked to come into the station. Other than the fact we were in the process of organising my father's funeral which was very protracted for various reasons I was not concerned as I felt it was natural that I would need to give an account of the incident. I left work early and met my mother at the station as she had wanted to come along. It was another incredibly hot day and we were left waiting for two hours in a boiling hot waiting room with no air conditioning with no explanation of why this was. We had been asked to attend voluntarily at a time which was not convenient. We asked on numerous occasions at the desk what the hold - up was we were told that we had to wait for a police officer to attend from another station to come over to take a statement. When finally we were seen the officers gave no explanation or apology and said that I was lying when I had said that we had not been told about the delay. They refused to allow my mother to accompany me into the interview and became very abusive to her. Once I had passed through the locked door they shouted in my face and refused to let me speak telling me that I was an adult and they would do what they liked.

One officer left to speak to the sergeant. Once he had left the other officer started shouting at me and told me that I had no right to speak in such a manner. When I pointed out that he had not even given me an opportunity to speak before he was insulting rude and disrespectful he then said that I was not to speak again until the interview. This I said I was more than happy about. I then entered the custody area without incident, we entered the incident room and they started to take details of the incident BEFORE the tapes were running so I pointed out that I was not prepared to speak until the tapes were running.

On at least five occasions they had told me that I was not under arrest and that I could have a solicitor present and that I was free to leave at any time. Once the interview was over I was asked to sign a piece of paper and when I asked what it was I was told it was the COVER for the tape but I was at no time made aware that this was in place of a written statement. As far as I was aware I was coming in to give a description of an accident which had occurred.

As we left the room I was told that I was being recorded for an offence of having a dog out of control in a public place. I was stunned as I wasn't aware that I was defending myself against any sort of crime. They then went on to inform me that they were now going to take my fingerprints, photograph and DNA. I questioned their right to do this as they had not told me that they had arrested me for anything and they said it was within their rights and that to be recorded was as good as an arrest and that they would use force if I refused. I said I wanted to speak to a solicitor first and they said that "if I was going to play that game" then they would take them right now as they had no time to wait! I questioned this and they told me they could do what they liked as they were the police. I asked if I could leave as I had been previously been advised that I could at any time. They refused and so I asked to speak to a solicitor once more as there was one standing within a few feet of me who was advising another individual at the police station. They merely shouted into my face told me not to raise my voice to them and that I would speak to a solicitor when it was convenient with them which would be AFTER they had forced me to have my DNA, fingerprints and photograph taken. Finally I was actually allowed to speak to a solicitor on the phone. He said he was amazed about how they were treating me but that they were legally able to do this.

Every police officer or solicitor I have spoken to subsequently has been horrified about the treatment I received but having read in the media about other incredible instances which have taken place in English police stations I am less surprised. I was warned not to make a complaint if I was concerned about my dog being destroyed, which was of course my only concern, but I have become irreversibly disillusioned about the behaviour of the police in England as a result of the treatment I received. I found their actions barbaric, unacceptable and a shameful way for a body REPRESENTING the public's interest to behave bearing in mind that English law as it stands is still INNOCENT UNTIL PROVEN GUILTY. This may not have broken the law as it stands but I feel that at a time when police image is at an –all-time low to compound it by this sort of yobbish behaviour is at best unfortunate and worst a very alienating tactic to the general public. I for one shall NEVER again, under any circumstances, enter a police station WITHOUT a solicitor present. Everyone I have spoken to about their behaviour has been appalled and I have been left genuinely anxious about ANY sort of police presence.

After this incident I heard nothing further and when I asked my solicitor if I should chase the situation up he said to do so under no circumstances. It was about two weeks later that I heard from a police officer in the area where the accident had happened and he said he wanted to come up and see how the dog was kept and to make recommendations for any future action. Obviously I was less than enthusiastic about dealing with any police officer again! He told me that he was very important and that the court would ultimately listen to his view on the situation. I spoke to my solicitor who said that I didn't have to allow the officer to visit but that it would be sensible to do so.

Finally FOUR weeks later he visited as he said it was complicated to arrange, we live 90 miles away! This was a dog which was supposed to be dangerous but it took four weeks to look into the situation. He was totally disinterested in the dog, he bordered on the verge of trying to chat me up and when that failed threaten me with what he could do to the dog if I didn't co-operate. He said that a doctor who had treated the child had written a statement to say that the injuries were the worst they had ever seen from a dog attack! This turned out to be one of his many lies. He said he had photographs to back this up, these included a small bruise to the arm where the dog had fallen on the child and a cut under her arm where the child fell on the stone. He finally left saying he would write a detailed important report to the court, again this was a lie, he made no report of his visit.

Once more after this stressful incident nothing more was heard. Six months later I received a letter from the court where the accident took place to say that I had to attend. Everyone, including my solicitor was amazed. If this was such a dangerous dog why had it taken six months to look into the case. I arrived at court and no information had been sent to my solicitor. He therefore asked for an adjournment which the magistrate was furious about. He accused my solicitor of delaying tactics until he pointed out that we had been totally unaware that the matter was going to court until two weeks previously. The magistrate then wanted to know from the prosecution why the matter had taken so long which she could not answer. The case was adjourned for a month for the prosecution to send information to my solicitor.

One week before the next hearing my solicitor had still received nothing. I had in the meantime taken Jake to a Behavioural psychologist to get him independently assessed. He behaved immaculately with everything that was thrown at him and the whole process was videoed. This was a costly exercise as was travelling and spending the night for each court case. When I arrived at court still my solicitor had seen no photographs of the child's injuries. I know he was getting anxious as he obviously was concerned that I might not have told him the whole situation as he had heard such worrying descriptions of what the bites(!) were like. In fact he was very relieved when he finally saw the photos and could not believe the case had gone so far.

My solicitor spoke to the prosecution and said that we would agree that Jake had hurt the child as a result of knocking her over but that we would not agree that he had attacked her. The prosecutor refused to consider this and said she wanted the dog destroyed even after all this time and having had no restrictions put on him. My solicitor then said that we would take the case to a Newton Hearing which was very rare but meant that I could plead guilty under The Dangerous Dog's Act but that I could contest how the injuries had occurred. Everyone I knew, particularly those with animals could not believe that I agreed to this as it was so obvious that Jake had not attacked the child but under the Act it doesn't matter how an injury was caused only that a dog in some way injured a person. The magistrates we had on this occasion clearly didn't like dogs. Whereas the initial magistrate had been annoyed with the incompetence of the prosecution these magistrates tried to blame my solicitor and what is worse they then tried to demand that the dog be seized and taken to police kennels. I could hear them arguing this and luckily the court clerk was pointing out that they didn't have the powers to do this. I have never felt so sick, I thought I would faint but I had decided that I was never going to hand him over to the police. The parting comment from the magistrates was that the case must be heard quickly and that I was to keep the dog under control!

There was another hearing planned in order to decide a date where everyone could be present at the hearing. I had to get a forensic scientist to analyse the injuries to the child and sent pictures of the stones at the beach as well as samples for him to look at. This of course was extra cost and thankfully he said he was happy that all this evidence demonstrated that the accident had occurred as I had explained. Everyone I spoke to had always argued that if a dog of Jake's size had attacked a child as the mother had described the child would be in pieces never mind a few scratches and bruises and one cut. At the next hearing the Newton Hearing was scheduled for another six months later. This then meant that it was eighteen months after the incident! No one could believe that there was to be a case arguing that a dog had to be destroyed after eighteen months because he was so dangerous!

I went through eighteen months of not being able to sleep and having stress-related health problems and I just wanted the case over with although the solicitor sensibly argued that it was good for Jake the longer the case went on. Finally the day came and I drove to the court at 4.00am to ensure I got there in time. I had taken Jake and Spotty to a safe house after my previous experience with the magistrates I wanted to take no chances that anything could happen to Jake. I didn't tell my solicitor but I intended to say that I had re-homed Jake if the outcome was bad. My solicitor told me when I arrived that if the worst came to the worst the magistrate could in fact seize the dog then and have him taken away even if went to appeal!

The mother of the child turned up for the first time on this occasion complete with a new-born baby. Now her older daughter was at school she would have had to work if she hadn't had another child. She ran in and out of doors to avoid looking at me. The dog psychologist and forensic scientist as well as my solicitor and a barrister had all turned up which was of course very expensive. My barrister then went to talk to the prosecution. It was a different solicitor now and my barrister returned saying he didn't understand but now the prosecution were not asking for the dog to be destroyed. It transpired that it was purely the mother who wanted Jake destroyed and that the prosecution solicitor was not prepared to take the case further as it was so clear from the defence evidence that it was purely an accident and no malice had been intended.

We were all called into court and the solicitors told the magistrates that we were coming to an agreement. The solicitors got together to talk over details and still the mother demanded that the Jake could not go out of the house without a muzzle and lead even at the farm and in the car! We would not agree to this but agreed that he would be taken to a public place without a muzzle and lead. I was furious afterwards that I had agreed to this as Jake had done nothing wrong but at the time I was just so relieved that he was not going to be destroyed. When we came back to court the magistrate seemed amazed that I had known the mother for a long time and she had accompanied me to the beach. I had explained my terrible financial situation due to the costs from the case and the strain it had put on me. She actually seemed quite sympathetic but I was fined £500 in total and given a criminal record. I was just thankful the dog was safe.

I have had my faith in human nature severely damaged and I have found it very difficult to get back on track after the multiple tragedies from the last two years but I am sure I will recover.

Chapter XI
Helga

Helga is a German Shepherd cross Border Collie, she came to The Alternative Animal Sanctuary as she had spent the first year of her life being starved and beaten and chained in a back yard in the middle of London. The RSPCA were called but as we have such inadequate animal welfare laws in the UK they said they could nothing for her. The next door neighbour could not stand to witness her pitiful life any longer so she took her but obviously could not keep her herself. Helga then went to this lady's friend who had young children, luckily Helga was good with the children but couldn't be taken out as she pulled on the lead and there was no where she could be off the lead. She was also so nervous of people because of her previous experience that her new owner was scared she would bite someone. Helga then had a third move in not even two years and stayed with the lady's estranged husband. He lived in a flat and worked long hours and so she was alone the whole the day and only taken out at night and so saw no one at all. Thankfully the gentleman realised that he could not continue keeping her in this environment and asked if I would have her. I was concerned how she would be with my other animals. I tried to persuade him to take her to Battersea Dogs Home as I had heard very positive things about them in recent years. He was worried to do so and having visited there recently I now think he was right.

Helga came up on a Sunday evening, which was the worst possible time as I had hoped to settle her in over the week end before I went back to work. She was also in season so she was attacking my dogs because they were annoying her. I was furious with the man and said that I ought to make him take her home. I did however realise that he was genuine and he really couldn't cope. Helga was skin and bone as he had never wormed her, she hadn't been vaccinated and obviously not spayed and she was exceptionally frustrated as she hadn't been getting enough exercise.

Initially life was pretty stressful, my other dogs were irritating Helga and she was retaliating. After a few weeks once she was out of season and she had been getting sufficient exercise she began to unwind. She was jumping every stable door in sight so I decided to enrol her in an agility club. She was an absolute nightmare she tried to bite the other dogs, the owners everything. I was very stressed as the case with Jake was –on-going and it was all quite a strain. I persevered and she got really good. She is a really intelligent dog and she loved the mental as well as physical activity. She really settled down with the other dogs and improved tremendously with people.

Bruno came to join us within a few months and he was a stray so I do not know his history but he was in a similar boat as Helga. He was lovely with people but clearly had suffered as Helga had with a lack of socialisation with other dogs so I started walking them together in order to see if they could learn from each other. Helga hated it as she was for the first time on the receiving end of her own behaviour! Helga however had the advantage in that she could run far faster than Bruno who was skin and bone and had no stamina. It only took about a week and they became firm friends and were inseparable. This was less good for Jake who they would bully but Spotty my little Jack Russell who had had a similar start as Helga would defend him and Bruno was pretty respectful of him! Eddie my elderly Rottweiler rescued from a drug dealer's house as a puppy liked to give encouragement on the –side-lines.

Everything really seemed to be moving forward well (always a bad sign) then just before Christmas Helga seemed very under the weather. I couldn't put my finger on it but she was tucked up and very low. I took her to the vet and she was very blasé and said she had hurt her back, she gave her a pain killer and said not to let her run around. She was in a lot of pain overnight and then in the early hours of the morning I realised that she could not move her back legs. I booked her into the vets first thing and asked for another vet to look at her, he said this was something which definitely needed surgery if she was to stand any chance of walking again. She was booked in at a nearby animal hospital that day and had £2000 of surgery carried out. The vets said that she had suffered an exploded disc and that there was no way of knowing why this had happened. It was particularly bad and had exploded with such force that is had effected six discs rather than the usual one or two.

I wondered whether the problem could have been due to her terrible treatment in early life or because she was taught to stand up on her back legs which she loved to do all the time to get attention, however much I tried to discourage her. No one can tell me and it will not help Helga anyway. I don't know if I did the right thing, I was unaware how long the healing process of spines take and I am looking into getting her a cart to increase her mobility as although she copes much better with her situation than I thought she would and I find it more upsetting than she seems to she is frustrated by the lack of exercise she can get.

Of course I don't know what the future holds but as is so often the case in my life I have seen from an animal how you can make the best of things. If someone had said to me that a dog so full of life, which had been treated so badly and was so active was going to end up like Helga was I would have said she couldn't have coped. Helga has proved me wrong and I am happy to be so.

Chapter XII

Birds

I have never been someone who can view animals in a hierarchical system as they all have equal intrinsic value to me. I have cared for many animals over the years and there are so many stories but some are more interesting to tell. On the bird front surprisingly one of the most memorable individuals was a pigeon called Petula. I had rescued a few pigeons from the vets where my sister worked as they had been injured and could not fly. Some were taken by a veterinary nurse down to Brownsee Island off the Dorset coast where there was a bird sanctuary but over the years I took in about six. Of all of them Petula became the biggest character. I had cared for them for a few years and they lived in the shed where the rabbits were kept. One day one named Peter flew out of the door which was open. Clearly he had recovered from his injury at this point! I was concerned about whether he would be able to survive in the wild as he had been a racing pigeon. I cut a hole in the wire which covered the window and within two hours he had returned! After that there was no stopping him or the others who followed and they would fly in and out of the window and sunbathe on the roof and were very happy.

This was an ideal situation as they got the opportunity to fly which was wonderful to watch and they still got their food on a plate so to speak. This also meant we no longer had to make trips to a wood about twenty miles away where there was no one who went shooting to release the many babies they produced over the years. It obviously was not acceptable to keep healthy babies captive but it was always a bit nerve-racking releasing them for the first time in case they couldn't fly well enough. There was however only one instance where we had to bring a baby back who was not sufficiently proficient.

The problem now was Petula who could not even get off the ground never mind fly and with the window open it was no longer safe enough to stay in the shed. I then made the decision to bring her into a touring caravan where I kept delicate animals of various species. She seemed quite happy but continually laid eggs which of course were never going to hatch! I thought then that it would be a good idea to give her a chicken egg to sit on. As it was so big for her she could only sit on one. This did in fact hatch and Oedipus was born! He was a white Silky cockerel so clearly not a pigeon. Thankfully neither of them minded about their obvious differences including the fact that Petula didn't need to feed Oedipus as she would have had to for her own pigeon chick. Petula and Oedipus remained devoted to each other hence his name and still when he was far too big he would try to sit underneath her with the result that she would be perched on his back!

I owned my first turkey after being asked to take him in because he had a friend and other chickens he lived with who had all been killed by a fox which he had fought against and clearly won! He was called Ollie and was probably the ugliest bird I had ever seen. He was delivered in a box and I opened it up to see a huge white bird with a revolting crest on his head which turned from bright red to bright blue and all the colours in between depending on his mood. He also had a disgusting black tassel of what looked like fur coming down from his chest. He was not a very friendly bird in fact he particularly hated men and would be quite aggressive in his demonstration of this. He could leave a nasty mark with a peck of his. For some reason he particularly liked to intimidate my father who as he got older and slower got quite nervous about him. Unfortunately about three months after my father died so did Ollie, I just hope he isn't still chasing him around now! The saving grace to Ollie was how he saved all of the chickens from a fox attack as he fought so hard and loudly that I discovered the situation in time and Ollie only had a small bite to his wing.

As I always hated animals being on their own I tried very hard to find some turkey friends for him. I only succeeded in this a few months before Ollie died of old age when I managed to rescue four from that year's Christmas dinner. Of the four I saved three died shortly before and after Christmas of heart attacks which I later found they are prone to because they are fed so many hormones and antibiotics as chicks. One survived to adulthood and I named her Olivia. She had a lovely nature and in fact all the females I got used to follow people around all the time. This was nearly Olivia's undoing as she was run over by a van. I came home from work and couldn't find her anywhere. After an hour or so I found her hidden in the hay stack where the driver had tried to cover up what he had done. I couldn't understand what had happened at first but she wouldn't come to me as usual. As I picked her up I found blood all over my hands and I thought initially that a dog had attacked her. I found a huge laceration in her neck and found out she had been trapped in the wheel arch of the van.

I was certain that she would not make it; I was amazed she had not already had a heart attack. I injected with her large quantities of antibiotics and cleaned out the wound and put large amounts of antiseptic cream in the wound rather as if I was stuffing her for Christmas lunch. I put her inside in the warm and decided the trauma of taking her to the vets would be too much and I couldn't see how they could stitch her up anyway. I couldn't believe that not only did she not get the wound infected but she also made a remarkably quick recovery. She didn't stop eating and once the wound had healed sufficiently I let her back out again. She was more reticent than previously but soon was back to her old self again just keeping a safer distance from traffic in the future.

There are many chicken stories but probably Muddle sticks out the best , she lived to be about eight years old and died of old age presumably. I couldn't be certain of her age as she was dumped in the neighbour's garden with two other chickens. She was the ugliest chicken I ever saw, a jet black game bird with a very long neck and a hideous head but a real character nonetheless. She had a funny walk about her but primarily she was desperate to hatch out chicks. Whatever she tried it always went wrong and nothing ever hatched for her. Finally I went to university for a week one summer and my mother and a young girl were left in charge. I phoned for my nightly check on the animals to absolute panic. All my mother kept saying was that there were now thirty more chicks as there were batches hatching everywhere and their mothers were bringing them home from every nook and cranny where they had been sitting all around the farm.

I arrived back home a couple of days later to find a very distressed Muddle as she had been sitting next door to one of the chickens who had hatched out a batch of chicks and in the confusion the other chicken had been given all of the chicks. Muddle was beside herself after all this time of desperately trying to hatch out her own chicks they had been taken from her. I couldn't stand it so against all text book advice I took a chick from one of the other hens and gave it to her. She was as 'pleased as Punch' hence he became Punch. Many of my chickens would share their chicks quite happily which generally people would say cannot happen as they would fight. Muddle however needed her own bit of space with her one much loved son. They remained inseparable for years which again is unusual as in general once the chicks have reached an annoying stage the mothers are pleased to see the back of them. Often I have hens who seem to remain bonded to their offspring permanently.

As with the turkeys I didn't have experience with geese until quite recently. I was given two by some people in Bath who could no longer keep them. They were sisters and very sweet. The first day proved to be very stressful as stupidly I let them go loose straightaway. They happily wandered around the fields but unexpectedly they proved to be very scared of the horses, which, finding them unusual, stampeded across the field and herded them into a corner. By the time I realised there was a problem I could only find one at the far end of the field. I searched for two hours but could see no sign of the other one, not even any feathers, etc. which I would have expected if a fox had got her.

I had given up any hope of finding her when still by nightfall there was no sign. Nevertheless the next day I drove around the lanes on my way to work and lo and behold about two miles away I found one goose calmly walking along the side of the road as if thumbing a lift. I stopped the car and followed her for a while until she would let me catch her. I put her on my lap while I drove home and then put her and her sister in the garden which was safely fenced in. They were so happy to see each other it made it all worthwhile. In the summer of that year both of the geese went broody even though only one has ever laid an egg to this day! I thought they would be very disappointed when nothing hatched so I brought some goslings and a ducking which I felt sorry for. I was told this would not work but although they seemed a little confused they were very happy.

One of the goslings I had brought had a developmental problem which became increasingly obvious as he grew older, I named him Mr Wobbly and he tried so hard. He was falling over more and more as time went on and then he just began to fade, I brought him in next to a heater but I wanted to keep him with the others as much as I could. Finally he lost his battle at a few months but he was so sweet that even in his short life he made a mark. As Ollie had gone by now the male baby, Gareth, had taken his guard duty to keep intruders (humans) at bay, but he was also to sound the alarm bell when the fox again got close to the chicken house trying to kill all the chickens.

Chapter XIII

Farm Animals

David, was my fist pig. I had always wanted a little, cute pink, cuddly pig. What I got was David, he was no Babe! He was enormous. I went to visit him at the farm where he lived. His owner had been a pig farmer but for some reason David had evaded slaughter over the years and now the owner was to lose the farm she was looking for a safe home for him.

I went with one of my sister's and my mother to get him transported. We had had a run and shelter built for him and we went in the sty, looked over and saw this twelve foot long gross white boar with huge tusks. I was beginning to feel sick. I was assured he was a really sweet pig and we 'just' had to get him out of the sty into the trailer. I didn't like to mention at this point that I was terrified! It took a good two hours of chasing David up and down and trying to persuade him to get into the trailer which finally we managed. Once we had unloaded him at the other end he seemed quite content with his new surroundings which were pretty luxurious compared to his sty. I soon got quite used to him although I avoided getting cornered in the back of the shelter with him blocking the exit if I could help it.

Probably the worst thing about David was that he had always been fed pig swill and that was all he would eat. His owner remained very dedicated to him until the end of his life years later and delivered the swill religiously each week. Boy did it smell. He actually was an affectionate pig and loved his ears being rubbed. At the end of his life he went off his back legs which meant I had to turn him regularly to stop him getting sore. I also had to clean him out more frequently as pigs really are very clean when they have the option. I was upset with his owner who would not agree to have him put down for two weeks as she was sure he would walk again which at twelve years old I really didn't think was going to happen. When the time finally came the knackerman wanted to drag him out of the shelter before shooting him but he relented and actually we ended up having to dismantle the front of his shelter so he could reach him without upsetting him.

One of the problems with pigs is that they get very stressed which means that they find moving surroundings hard to cope with, when I later adopted two Vietnamese Pot Bellied pigs who were sisters I had to move them from the enclosure they had been in for years, this was to prove very traumatic for all concerned as they would scream, I would be worried they were going to get a heart attack and despite their round shape they could move very fast. I owned a number of pigs over the years as it was a bit of 'the old woman who swallowed the fly' scenario. David had had the company of a Pigmy goat for a while named Harry. A lady had asked if he could stay as she had nowhere to put him. He was actually very human-friendly so frequently escaped to be with human company. It was, then, good for him when he moved to the lady's house but then David was on his own and he had become fond of Harry. That was why I didn't like getting involved with other people and their animals, as I had explained before Harry came to stay that I didn't want David upset. As a result I had to go and buy another pig in the form of Reggie a Pot Bellied Pig. Reggie was tiny and a baby and I was so worried David would hurt him but they got very attached to each other and when David died Reggie went to live with the two sisters. Finally both sisters died so I had to find another companion for Reggie, along came Sharon. She was enormous, a local farmer had not wanted to slaughter her and said I could have her and that she wasn't very big!

Sharon came during the Foot and Mouth crisis so masses of paperwork was necessary. She arrived and my mother was horrified and demanded the farmer take her back. Thankfully he said he couldn't and Reggie was very happy with her as he could snuggle right into her huge tummy. They were later joined by Powerpack the goat who was to be fed to the local pack of hounds as a children's farm had bred too many goats and didn't want him. He dragged me the length of the farm as he was so strong, hence his name. Later when I took in some more goats I hoped Powerpack would live with them but he had no desire in this plan and chose to stay with his pig friends.

Chapter XIV
Small Animals

I must confess that over the years I have made mistakes with small animals despite my best efforts. I have always wanted them to have space and freedom and even though I have tried to keep them safe I they have escaped and through ignorance of their needs and behaviours I have had avoidable accidents. Of course I have tried to learn from my mistakes but that does not help the ones who suffered and for that I am very sorry. I have had the pleasure of knowing some wonderful little, and not so little characters.

One of my most notorious rabbits was Oddie, his mother, Bright-eyes, had been owned by a family where the children were left with sole responsibility for her. As the name suggests she was the victim of the rabbit craze from the Watership Down film. I visited the house and was taken to see her in her empty cage where she was skin and bone. I then pestered the young boy who had a soft spot for me to let me have her. I brought her home and got her out every hour or so to let her have a few nibbles of grass as I was so worried she may explode if given too much food when she clearly wasn't used to it. We always got on well which unfortunately was not the case with my mother and her and when she, on the rare occasion, had to feed Bright-eyes she would attack my mother quite viciously. I got her back to full health.

I am ashamed to say it now but I used to breed from the rabbits to sell, primarily because I loved the babies but also because it gave me some pocket money. I think in general they went to good homes but I am sure some didn't and that is my responsibility and there is no way to escape that. Bright-eyes had her first litter and would not take to it and Oddie was the result. As she had rejected him we set about hand-rearing him in the same way we had reared orphaned kittens. We knew nothing about this and realised only when it was too late that the kitten milk we had used was not suitable and he developed rickets. He was such a character and went on to drink from his bottle until he was quite a few months old. When he was a year or so we moved house and all the rabbits could be moved from living in rabbit hutches. They were quite spacious but cages all the same. At the new property there were a range of pig sties which were lovely and big although there was not as much natural light as there should have been.

Oddie loved his new environment and he was unbothered by his splayed out legs as he was able to manoeuvre himself perfectly well, if a little unorthodoxly. He lived until a reasonable age of about eight with no further health problems much to everyone's amazement. Once again proving that animals can overcome disability if given the opportunity. His mother also lived to a good age and after one more litter of twenty babies she never had any more as she was clearly not the maternal type. One of her neighbours had jumped the wall and mated her unbeknown to me as he had jumped back once the deed was done, she was obviously not very welcoming. It was probably just as well that such an enormous litter did not survive as that would have been a handful to hand rear! It was nonetheless tragic.

Paddington was another character who had a very sad life. As I said, I now regret the fact that I bred rabbits if but only for a few years. I especially regret that I used to take some of the babies back to the breeder I brought my original rabbits from to sell as she was very well known. She later gained a very bad reputation for the terrible conditions she kept her rabbits in as she got too old to care for them. I knew her well before this stage but even so she was getting more business orientated already which was when I stopped have contact with her.

On one visit I made I saw a tiny square cage with triple wire on the front so that you could barely see in. When I enquired about this she said the rabbit had been sold by her and had run loose on a farm, the owners then wanted to breed from him as he was of good quality and so put him in a cage and then were surprised when he was too vicious to handle. I felt so sorry for him as he paced (the two paces he could manage in his tiny cage) backwards and forwards. He was desperate and reminded me of the film Roots I watched as a child about Africans captured and enslaved and chained up. They went mad with the confinement. I decided I wanted to have him and in true business style she sold him to me despite his 'worthless' monetary value. I brought him home and put him in a pig sty. He went running round and round for a good long time until he realised that he was going to have the space to move now. I would have liked him to have more space but I needed to put a lid on his run in case he jumped out and I couldn't catch him again and he got attacked by anything.

He lived quite a short life but I would like to feel a much happier one. The saddest thing was that the only time I could hold him to cuddle him was at the very end when he was partially paralysed by a stroke. I had him put down and don't know whether the stroke was to do with his stressful incarceration or just bad luck!

Out of the little rodent animals I had I remember a particular group of gerbils and hamsters I had at once. I had two Syrian hamster males who lived happily together which I had never heard of before and they were really wonderful, Tommy and Timmy (named by my nephews). I was encouraging my nephews to get interested and take responsibility for animals and as they were not allowed any of their own they came to visit and play with the gerbils and hamsters. We used to get them all out together and let them run around which they were very content with. The gerbil was called James and they were really special little souls. Sadly my nephews grew out of any interest in animals when they got interested in posh clothes, video games etc. but for that year or so they did get a lot of enjoyment and understanding from these little creatures.

Chapter XV

The Riding School

I had always sworn that I would never put my horses into a riding school. I had seen too many over-worked, under fed and physiologically damaged by it. This was to be a promise I couldn't keep. I hated every minute of it initially but I did find quite early on that I could actually do quite well for the horses. No one has ever been able to carry whips. I have never made a horse get up when it is lying down to go out for a ride, I do not allow yanking in the mouth or booting in the sides and I think in general the horses have enjoyed it and found it less stressful than I have. I also have to say that I have for the most part met some very nice people. I have encouraged people who are interested in animals and their care and welfare to come to the school rather than the true 'riding people' who I am not much fond of.

It is noted as being pretty 'Alternative'. It is more often than not that there are a few horses wandering around loose and head collars are rarely seen. I find it strange that horses for some reason, who are after all one of the least aggressive, most malleable of animals, spend their time being tied up or boxed in stables. Mine come in and out loose, they know which stables they 'should' go in and in most cases they do. They can all touch each other over the stable walls as they are only three feet high and those who are too small share a stable in pairs. I feel it is very important for all animals to have a special pair bond as I believe it helps their physical and psychological health. I aim for the horses to go out on rides with their respective partners but they are in any event certainly never separated from their friends for long periods of time. To the average horse 'expert' my stables break every rule there is yet the horses seem happy and everyone who visits notes the relaxed atmosphere which is probably why when I visit other yards I find it so stressful.

Actually The Riding School has been relatively uneventful through the years. This is of course the aim. I have had three serious accidents in twelve years, two were with people who insisted on riding horses I told them not to ride in situations I told them not to get into. One was also diabetic which she had never mentioned and she reacted very badly which took me by surprise. That surprise was not as great as the fact that the ambulance men refused to carry her out of the bridle path and made her get back on the horse and ride a mile's distance when she was clearly very unwell. Another accident occurred when joy riders were driving down a bridle path into the horses and caused them to bolt and a lady to fall on about the only razor-sharp stone on the entire mile length of the bridle way!

Certainly the most stressful was the loss of one of the horses during a ride. I had been told as a child how one of my uncles in Germany had been riding a horse which had served in the I World War and it dropped down dead underneath him and how traumatic that was. I have since heard of other cases but it is obviously rare and not what you plan for. We were out on a ride and I had rescued a 16.2hh Thoroughbred Sam, a few years earlier who had been worked physically very hard until his tendons broke down and then had gone to a home where he was near starved. I had taken him on as a skeleton. He was a very kind horse and devoted to another horse Baxter not least because his eyesight was poor so he tended to follow him around. After months of work and very expensive feeding he began to get back to his old handsome self (he was actually now in his twenties but amazingly looked far younger). He was a very strong ride and one of the girls who rode at The School was particularly fond of him, she was quite big and not a good rider but Sam seemed to like her and I had to have someone who could manage him. We went on one of the usual rides as there are not many to choose from. At certain points the horses know that is the place to canter as there are only certain places where it is safe. We rounded the corner before the canter and then all set off. Sam unusually was further behind and as we got to the top of the hill we heard a cry from the rider and I turned to see Sam and her fall to the ground. Thankfully the rider was thrown clear and didn't end up trapped underneath as can happen. I jumped off my horse and I think instinctively knew what was happening. I yelled at her to get clear as Sam was thrashing his legs wildly about. I got up to him as he stopped moving and tried to calm the rider down. I explained it must have been a heart attack and that he would have been dead before he even hit the ground. The movement was nerves not conscious movement and he wouldn't have suffered.

I arranged for the horses and riders to get safely back to the stables and for Sam's body to be removed. I was comforted by the fact that the slaughtermen asked if he was a young horse as he looked so good! When a post mortem was performed it was found that he actually had an aneurysm which could have ruptured at any time. It was traumatic for everyone involved and Baxter couldn't understand why Sam never returned but for Sam I think it was the way he would have been happy to go.

Chapter XVI

Becoming a charity

It was only after I had been rescuing animals for over twenty years that I realised I really did need more financial support, not least economic aid. I had been introduced to the internet at work and felt that a website would be a good start. Having looked into what was needed myself I realised that it was beyond my present capabilities and so I advertised on an excellent site called Animal Rescuers for someone who would be prepared to help me set up a website. I was very surprised to have so many offers and so needed to make a decision as to who to 'choose'! It went some way to restore my faith in human nature having found people who were prepared to help for no financial reward. As it turned out I made an exceptionally good choice in the form of John Beale. He actually was in a difficult situation at the time himself but said that he was prepared to give me –on-going support even once the site was up and running and he has been as good as his word

.

The animal sanctuary website was born at **www.alternativesanctuary.co.uk**. Everyone was very impressed by the professional look and it only took a year until

200+ visitors were accessing a day. Then came the next stage. It was unfortunately not bringing in any money as yet but it was attracting the attention of more owners who couldn't or didn't want their animals anymore and they were coming from nation-wide. I looked at other sites who sold merchandise and at the same time I was looking for specialist products I needed for some of the animals I had at The Sanctuary and so I thought I would look at importing exclusive goods from abroad. I came across some good products manufactured in The States and approached the owners who for the most part were very keen to do business with me and gave me exclusive rights for selling their products in Europe. From this was born **www.alternativepetshop.co.uk** The biggest snag I have hit is that the advertising for a business is so expensive so that at present the venture is not paying off and I do not have the capital to invest to expand. I do not intend to give up. Apart from the fact that I cannot afford to do so I have not so far given up on something even if it begins as an uphill struggle.

I looked into many of the 'get rich quick schemes' which of course are not genuine and prey on the most desperate and vulnerable. I will stick with the 'old fashioned' method of working hard to succeed but of course this takes time, which I am limited with in both the aspect of fitting everything in each day and for the fact that finances are running out for the future. I have started up a small and non-expensive set up business in the form of The Alternative Cleaning Business. I find cleaning quite therapeutic and I have specialised in the houses of pet owners who find it particularly hard to get people to clean and who are happy to let themselves in the house when the dogs are there. So far this has been slow but expanding. To a large extent it relies on personal recommendation and in the winter months I have limited time so I am hoping to concentrate on this area more fully over the summer months. I would like to expand into the education area and design courses (of a higher standard than at present exist) and to tutor adults and children but this is not off the ground as yet.

Essentially my mind is open to any opportunity and publicity is the greatest need. The double edged sword is that the more well known The Sanctuary gets the more animals I tend to acquire rather than necessarily raising more money. I am battling through the minefield of becoming a registered charity to enable me to find more avenues of financial aid, to increase confidence in the legitimacy of The Sanctuary and because you are limited as to the amount of money you are legally allowed to raise otherwise. One of the biggest problems is not only the paper work and legal issues involved but also that you have to have raised £10,000 before you can be considered! My present mission is to get fundraising!!

Chapter XVII

The Animal Behaviour Business

I have always had a desire for study and as there were no animal courses on offer until recently I have studied various subjects and found this mentally stimulating and rewarding. Essentially my life has always consisted of caring for my animals so my only diversion from this has been study (sad I know). I also obviously have time constraints and am someone who likes to work on their own so I have relied in the main on distance learning courses. I have to be honest and say that this has also resulted in a large degree of disappointment as I have found so little standardisation in what is available. I have studied with five colleges and have found with the exception of two that in the main they are handing out material of very low quality and often of limited accuracy.

It also leads on to my experience of the many animal behaviourists who have sprung up in recent years with no credibility. It is very much a case of 'suck it and see'. The most worrying aspect is that the animals are the ones to suffer. You can hear the same terminology recited over and over again. People tend to latch on to a particular concept which has been 'discovered' and they adopt it and teach that it will 'cure all ills'. I have a grave worry that we will see the problems which will arise from this way into the future.

What really amazes me is that so many 'experts' have so little 'hands on' experience, they read a few books and with total conviction go out on to the unsuspecting public to give advice and treatment with the result that often problems are made far worse and can result in the animal's destruction. They really are playing with these animals' lives.

I would say that the important point of animal care and so behaviour is consistency, boundaries, patience, understanding and of course love and respect. Don't ask for perfection, accept what you are given and be grateful for it. THINK before you acquire an animal; think about what their needs and traits are, not want your ideal is.

Chapter XVIII
Animal Job Searches

As I was growing up I always wanted to work with animals and I was told not to as I wouldn't want to do it all day and then come home to do mine in the evenings, it's badly paid and long hours. I have now got to the point in my life where I have tried a variety of different things but I now know it is animals I want to be with. I wouldn't change the past I have learnt a lot and I am not sure I was ready to work with animals full-time before. I have gone through different stages before I reached here. On my quest however I have had the opportunity to go to a variety of organisations, big and small for interviews and to look around.

In general I have to say I have not been that impressed by the bigger organisation (any organisations including charities) when they get bigger and more money they seem to lose their focus or their original aim. Large amounts of money is raised but there seems a reluctance to spend it on direct animal rescue work. There are of course exceptions. I was very impressed with The Mayhew Animal Centre in London where they have a small set up but it is the most relaxed I have been to. A lot of care has been put into the design of the cat and dog housing so that the animals were in very peaceful surroundings which can only be beneficial certainly for their psychological well-being. In my opinion not enough importance is placed on the very stressful environment especially the large rescue centres create. Any dog without a behavioural problem initially will soon develop one in this situation and their true personality can never be brought out.

There are an increasing number of organisations who pride themselves on the fact that they do not put animals down, this then begs the question whether it is right for dogs to spend years in kennels instead. There are equally many thousands possibly going into the millions of animals who are destroyed when given the right circumstances this would not be necessary. Many 'sanctuaries' are still hell holes, the animals stand no chance and money is the true motivator. In fact although I think rescued animals should be paid for if for no other reason than it makes people realise that they have worth and that all animals need a lot of forethought for the commitment and financial requirements they have. There is certainly, though, a case to keep a check on the sums of money charged if for no other reason it helps to fuel the dog theft trade because people look for cheaper alternatives.

Chapter XIX

The Story So Far

At the time of writing the story so far looks very bleak, with a string of tragedies one after another I have debts of £40,000 to clear and no possibility of borrowing more to continue to feed the animals. Of course I can tell myself, it's only money if the animals are well that is the main thing which it is but that will not continue without the financial means I need. Despite the UK's reputation as a nation of animal lovers this is sadly not born out in reality with cruelty, neglect and abandonment cases on the increase there are too many animals and nowhere for them to go never mind the wider issues of factory farming, vivisection etc.

My belief in life is that if things are meant to be they will be, in general things often do work out for the best and just when things can't seem any bleaker there is a light but at the moment it is more like a miracle I am waiting for.

I leave you in 2004 you may want to find out how things progress from here in the next book in the series.

Join me during the really tough times and the better times and follow the sanctuary's onward progress.